Humanistic Approach to Psychotherapy

Humanistic Approach to Psychotherapy

Eric Whitton
Humanistic Psychotherapist, London

with six contributors

Whurr Publishers
London

© 2003 Whurr Publishers Ltd
First published 2003
by Whurr Publishers Ltd
19b Compton Terrace
London N1 2UN
England

British Library Cataloguing in Publication Data

A catalogue record for this book is available from the British Library.

ISBN 1 86156 300 0

Typeset by Adrian McLaughlin, a@microguides.net
Printed and bound in the UK
by Athenæum Press Ltd, Gateshead, Tyne & Wear.

Contents

Preface

What is humanistic psychotherapy? This book attempts to answer that question. Its main purpose is to describe, rather than to define, what humanistic psychotherapy is commonly understood to cover and its distinctive place in the world of psychology and therapeutic practice, and to advocate its benefits for a wide range of problems that people face in this age of anxiety.

As the title of this book indicates, humanistic psychotherapy is an *approach* to the practice of psychotherapy. It has a set of beliefs and practices but it consists of a group of disciplines that combine a variety of theoretical models.

In the growing complexity of what is being offered to the public, it is timely and important to write an exposition of this approach, sometimes called the third force in psychology. When individuals without a great deal of information decide to go into therapy or to embark upon training, they usually have little idea that there is such a large range of methods available; yet, although all therapists seek to assist people in dealing with their lives, there are many ways in which they differ both in theory and in practice.

Many people, both professional and lay, are not aware of the different forms of therapy. There is psychoanalysis, originated by Freud and developed into different schools by Jung, Adler, Klein and others. This is sometimes referred to as psychodynamic psychotherapy. The main aim of this discipline is make contact with the unconscious as a way to gain insight into what drives people to do and feel what seems to be out of their control. Then there is behavioural psychotherapy, which, as its name implies, focuses on changing the way people behave rather than how they feel. It is structured and directive with clear time limits.

Within the *humanistic* approach there are three crude divisions, which have their starting point with the body, mind or spirit. It is not the purpose of this book to define what any given school of therapy practises or preaches but I shall draw out, from this wide body of disciplines, what they seem to have in common. Not all will agree with this view but it is hoped that most will accept most of it as a reasonable account of the scope of humanistic practice.

Another aim of this book is to provide a common-sense approach to the field of therapy that is non-partisan and at the same time open to contradiction. This, I believe, gives the best possibility for development. The world of psychotherapy today is plagued by the almost compulsive urge to be regarded as 'kosher' in one sense or another. The reason for this is that there is no given authority like the British Medical Council that can define adequately or control what is a proper psychotherapist or what is not.

The climate that prevailed in the early years of the humanistic movement avoided labels – diagnostic labels or labels to define status. Some of the early pioneers refused to call themselves 'psychotherapists' because they thought that this restricted what they were offering. What they offered was not only more than could be categorized as psychotherapy but it also didn't make claims to offer a cure – rather, it claimed to provide the possibility for growth and resolution within the client's stated interest.

Although I do not want to avoid controversy in this book, I would rather say what, from my experience, humanistic psychotherapy *is* rather than what it *is not*. One of the characteristics of those who call themselves humanistic is the inclusiveness of their approaches. Clearly there are some theoretical and idealistic grounds for espousing the humanistic cause, but I am sure that many of those who would not call themselves humanistic in this sense, in fact practise some aspects of the humanistic approach. It is not for me to go into any detail about them, as my knowledge of other approaches is second or third hand. What I am trying to say in these introductory remarks is that all therapists, and indeed all people working in the helping professions, are there for the benefit of those they serve. It is primarily *how* they set about it and secondarily *what* they think they are doing that is likely to differ if they are humanistically orientated. I dearly want to avoid drawing tight lines of demarcation. What is needed at present is not a doctrinal statement or a manual but an exposition that leads to further discussion of this approach.

Terminology

This book is mainly aimed at the helping professions to give an argument for humanistic therapy, as well as those in training. It is written in such a way as to make it accessible to lay people who might not be aware of the place of humanistic therapy within the service available to them in their personal and emotional lives as well as within the work and family setting. The aim is to show its distinctive contribution, its range of competence and wide application, and to avoid making invidious comparisons with other approaches.

Humanistic psychology, then, is a body of theory accumulated from the main contributors to the humanistic potential movement, which began in the 1960s. The *human potential movement* was a new and alternative development, which took a new and different attitude to helping people – an attitude that was non-authoritarian, positive and personally empowering.

Humanistic psychotherapy is the professionalization of these ideas by a loosely defined group of practitioners who either see their roots in the early stages or who find the term useful to distinguish them from other forms of psychotherapy. The use of the word *psychotherapy* includes counselling, training and any forms of practice that might be described as therapeutic. The terms *therapist* and *psychotherapist* are used interchangeably. *Humanistic psychotherapist* is used to create a distinction from other kinds of psychotherapists.

In order to avoid the impersonal use of inclusive gender-neutral words to describe people, I have used the masculine pronoun to indicate the therapist and the feminine pronoun to indicate the client.

Structure

In *Part One* of this book, you will find the story of the humanistic movement up to the present day. Its purpose is to show what brought about this social movement, which most of Western society has experienced. To most readers under 40 this period will be something that their parents talked about. Nevertheless, much of what we take for granted today – personal freedom, a belief in love, and care about the way we treat each other, was given a new meaning all those years ago. Those who consider the affairs of everyman and the sharing of power to be important will identify with the developments of the humanistic movement and what it stands for today.

This overview is followed, in *Part Two,* by a description of the significant aspects of humanistic theory and practice. Without going into detail about these topics, the reader is given a broad picture of the essence of humanistic beliefs and the way in which humanistic psychotherapy is carried out.

Part Three highlights some of the major issues for humanistic psychotherapy and indeed for any form of therapy. In seeking to hold together the polarities implicit in the principles and practice of psychotherapy, the humanistic approach maintains a balance between the different positions.

Humanistic psychotherapy covers such a wide and diverse number of disciplines that it is hard to draw lines of distinction between them. For this reason, in *Part Four,* a number of practitioners from various backgrounds have been invited to describe how they view their approach to psychotherapy within the humanistic framework. This diversity is well summed up in the introduction to the UK Association of Humanistic Psychology Practitioners (UKAHPP) Core Beliefs Statement:

The humanistic approach to psychology and therapy cannot be summarised in one single definition. The humanistic view is one of 'many ways of looking', in that root knowledge of oneself, of others and of the world is based essentially on inner experience and experiential encounter with others and with the world. Hence humanistic theories of what it is to be a person are of necessity varied; there are different maps but none is the actual territory. Accordingly this statement of AHPP's beliefs presents a variety of views, divided into two sections. Firstly fundamental beliefs, the tenets of humanistic psychology, to which all humanistic practitioners would subscribe in varying degrees. Secondly a range of views from which the practitioner can select those they experience to be true, putting the others aside rather than rejecting them. (UKAHPP Handbook, 2003, p. 5)

Finally, in *Part Five* there is a summary of the present position of the humanistic approach and a discussion of its possible future directions.

The nature of humanistic psychology

Humanistic psychology has its orgins in a number of different sources including the practice of medicine, research into human behaviour in groups large and small, education and training, and social work. One of its features was the rejection of what is called the 'medical' model, which was regarded as prescriptive and centred on the expertise of the professional. Therefore, what followed, to a greater or lesser extent, was client centred, a term coined by Carl Rogers to describe this change of emphasis. It was not so much that 'the customer is always right' as 'the therapist is not always right'. His premise was that the client (not patient) knows far more about herself than any expert. She may not be aware of a lot about herself. She may not understand herself. However, as she becomes more self-aware and develops a sense of responsibility for herself, she is likely to know what her needs are, what she can change, and what she is willing to change. So the therapist and the client are engaged in a process on equal terms. This is the most important aspect of humanistic psychotherapy.

Since the establishment of humanistic methods in the field of personal development, much of what issued out of the humanistic movement went on outside the realms of psychotherapy. Teaching methods began to change their orientation and became, at least in primary schools, more pupil centred. In secondary schools I was involved in a national careers guidance project, which started with employment needs rather than 'schooling'. This, in turn, led to a more student-orientated curriculum in the training of teachers. Training courses invited participants to contribute their learning needs, which in some cases became the 'agenda' for the course. When I was a trainer, I can remember the surprise from trainees at actually being asked by an expert what they would like to deal with. Now, as a psychotherapist, I rarely meet this kind of response. Often such an approach seems to be expected, which is an indication of how widespread this change in emphasis has become. The introduction of supervision in the social work field implied the need for social workers to provide support in their involvement in their clients' problems rather just doling out what was thought to be good for them. We have also seen a much greater emphasis in business on customer consultation. It is my contention that the spread of humanistic principles has grown far beyond the limits of psychotherapy. It also includes the increasing importance attached to the value of psychological consultants in industry, sport and politics.

For me personally, writing this book has been a voyage of rediscovery and an opening of new doors that has been a rich and rewarding experience. It has reminded me of the path that I have travelled with others in my growth as a person and practitioner. I have had some personal contact with most of what I have written about directly or through indirect contact with others who have told me about their experience. I have come to my present understanding and position through experiencing most of the humanistic methods, starting back in the late 1960s. I have been involved in the application of humanistic principles in the Church, in youth work and education, in hospitals, as well as in the field of counselling and therapy. I trust that you, the reader, will catch some of the passion that lies at the heart of humanistic beliefs and practice.

Acknowledgements

The people to whom I feel a sense of gratitude for all that I have gained and learned in this field of endeavour are far too numerous to mention, apart from a few outstanding mentors and friends, some of whom are no longer alive: David Manship, who introduced me to inductive learning, and the radical group of colleagues I encountered through him in the General Synod Board of Education; Alan K Rice of the Tavistock Institute with whom I had my first experience of T-Groups; Reg Batten of the Institute of Education, University of London, who taught me non-directive methods; Eugene Heimler who showed me how to make co-operative assessments with clients; John Southgate of the former North London Polytechnic, who helped me unlearn everything I thought I knew; Eoin O'Leary, a gestalt teacher, who lived life to the full without guilt; Michael Reddy, Bob Goulding, Emily Ruppert and especially Alice Stevenson who, through Transactional Analysis, taught me how to be a psychotherapist by example as well as by word; the various psychotherapists with whom I worked over a period of 12 years in a variety of disciplines – encounter, bioenergetics, psychosynthesis, gestalt, biodynamic, as well as hundreds of hours in training groups of all kinds. I have met some remarkable people whom I count as friends. I am grateful for those who supported me in the writing of this book, particularly Judy Graham, Maria Gilbert and Ian Mackrill, who have read through drafts and made valuable comments.

I have also gained from many colleagues, including the members of the Open Centre, where I have been a member for over 20 years; students and colleagues on the humanistic counselling courses at Roehampton Institute; the members of the Association of Humanistic Psychology Practitioners with whom I have worked with for 10 years as ethics officer, chair and general secretary, and who have helped me more than I can say on my humanistic journey; the staff of the London Bridge Hospital and the other hospitals in the group, where I am teaching clinical supervision, who have shown a quality of commitment and human kindness that has been a pleasure. And last, but not least, I must add to this long list so many of my clients and students who have shown me, over the past 25 years, what it is to be human in many different ways.

Contributors

Maria Gilbert is a chartered clinical psychologist, integrative psychotherapist, trainer and supervisor who has many years of experience in adult education, organizational consultancy and training and who also maintains a private psychotherapy and supervision practice. She is currently head of the integrative psychotherapy, integrative counselling psychology and psychotherapy, and supervision courses at Metanoia Institute in west London. Her most recent publication is *Psychotherapy Supervision* (2000) co-authored with Kenneth Evans.

Judy Graham is a member of the UK Association of Humanistic Psychology Practitioners (UKAHPP) and the Association for the Advancement of Gestalt Therapy. She trained in London at the Metanoia Institute and the Gestalt Centre. Based in London, she works both in private practice and in the National Health Service primary care health centres. She also works with organizations, conducts research in interprofessional learning, supervises complementary therapists working with immune-related diseases, and trains counsellors and social workers in primary care settings.

Julie Hewson is the founder and senior partner of the Iron Mill Institute in south-west England. She has been in practice for over 20 years and is fascinated by the tapestry of thinking, culture, life experiences, literature, history and art as well as psychotherapy in mapping the journey human beings have in their encounters with universal dilemmas, relationships, and dragons. She works in Prague, Dublin, Zurich, Granada and Naples and combines a range of theoretical approaches in her work including transactional analysis, integration and humanistic therapy, as well as artistry and humour.

David Jones received a degree in psychology after doing his national service. He worked in Africa for three years and was a university teacher at the London School of Economics for 25 years, during which time he began training as a humanistic and integrative group facilitator and psychotherapist. A chartered psychologist and a graduate of the Karuna Institute, he is accredited by the UKAHPP and registered with the United Kingdom Council for Psychotherapy (UKCP). He has contributed to a number of publications, edited *Self and Society* for a number of years, and edited *Innovative Therapy; A Handbook* for the Open University Press. He lives and works in south London.

Jochen Lude has been working for over 20 years as a body psychotherapist. He has integrated several approaches in his work, having studied body psychotherapy with various leading teachers, and is also a qualified transpersonal psychotherapist. Before he trained as a psychotherapist, he worked in Berlin as a community organizer, activating people and enabling them to organize themselves to improve their living conditions. In 1983 he co-founded the Chiron Centre for body psychotherapy in London, where he has been a trainer, supervisor and managing director ever since. He also maintains a private practice there. In his work he is especially interested in how therapists can use their own bodies as sounding boards in the interaction with their clients.

Eric Whitton was a parish priest for six years and then spent twelve years as a training officer in community education with the Church of England and as director of the London Training Group, where he was responsible for training trainers in group work. He has undergone extensive training in transactional analysis and has experience of a variety of humanistic methods. He has been in practice as a psychotherapist in London and a member of the Open Centre since 1980. For the past ten years he has been on the board of Association of Humanistic Psychology Practitioners – formerly as chair and currently as general secretary. For seventeen years he was course tutor in humanistic counselling at Roehampton Institute. At present, he is working with a London group of hospitals as a consultant in clinical supervision. He also runs summer workshops in Italy. He has written a book on his approach to therapy called *What is Transactional Analysis?*

Courtenay Young is an accredited psychotherapist living and working at the Findhorn Foundation. He is also a regional co-ordinator for Scotland for the Spiritual Emergence Network and teaches modules on spiritual emergence to psychotherapy training centres. He has just written a handbook for people experiencing spiritual emergencies – and people working with those who are experiencing them – entitled *First Contacts with People in Crisis.*

PART ONE
THE HUMAN POTENTIAL MOVEMENT

Chapter 1
Background and origins

It is not easy to establish clearly the origins of humanistic psychotherapy. The movement could be traced far back into history to the Eastern and Greek philosophers, through the early Church, the Renaissance, the Reformation and the Enlightenment. One could also include the American and French Revolutions and Marxism in this historical review as movements that were about the rights and place of ordinary people in the world order. The human potential movement, however, began alongside the changes that were taking place in Western society in the 1940s and 1950s.

Much earlier than that, in the 1920s, Jacob Moreno was practising psychodrama – a method for re-enacting life situations. His inventive ideas about helping people to be involved in their own therapy were the precursor of humanistic methods. Using his highly active techniques to solve problems, with his emphasis on spontaneity and creativity, his work became a major resource. However, for many years his work was not accepted.

Following the Second World War, and through the 1950s, there was a considerable, if gradual, change in many of the accepted norms in society. Alongside this was a growing optimism that resulted from the reaction to the awful atrocities of the Second World War. People felt they had fought for something – to make a better world – and there was a generally felt need to create an optimal environment in which it would be possible for everyone to grow.

The early 1960s saw the burgeoning of a worldwide movement that could be labelled 'alternative'. In his book *The Making of a Counter Culture*, Theodore Roszak (1971) explored the issues that caused the change in social consciousness that was taking place. This change challenged the traditional attitudes of people towards authority. Youthful opposition, embodied in the counterculture, insisted on the right of people, as individuals and groups to make choices for themselves. This was expressed in pop music, dress, drug culture and sexual liberation. Alongside this there was a questioning of authority and disillusionment with the establishment, which had clearly failed in the eyes of younger people: 'the young – those born after 1940 – find themselves living in a society that neither commands nor deserves respect' (Chiaromonte, 1968, pp. 25–7). War came to be seen as a useless

waste of life. Ordinary people began to realize that they could have an
effect on political and social decision-making. The presence of John
Kennedy in the White House, who was beginning to challenge the power
of big business, and his quest for peace, inspired many younger people to
believe they were not alone in their hopes for a more humane society.
Civil disobedience began to be the means whereby demands for radical
change could be heard. This surfaced in protest movements against the
dehumanizing forces of war and nuclear weapons – movements epitomized by the Campaign for Nuclear Disarmament, the Aldermaston
marches, the student uprising in Paris, the riots in Grosvenor Square
against the war in Vietnam, and the civil rights movement. In social and
personal spheres people questioned the accepted moral standards.
Sexual freedom for both men and women resulted in women's liberation,
the gay movement, beatniks, the beat generation, hippies, experiments
with drugs and a breaking out of the restrictions imposed by the older
generation. At the same time the reaction to tradition was being
expressed most vividly in the folk, beat and rock music of Elvis Presley,
Pete Seeger, the Beatles, Bob Dylan, and many others. Alternative writers
were influenced by Zen, like Jack Kerouac who first came up with the
label 'the beat generation', Timothy Leary who researched altered states
of consciousness through LSD, the mystic Alan Watts, the poet Allen
Ginsberg, and the novelist William Burroughs. The movies *The Graduate*
and *Easy Rider* reflected different aspects of the change in the values of
young middle-class people. The family was under threat.

It is often thought that teenagers sowed the seeds of dissonance.
Originally, however, it was adults, students and intellectuals, for the
most part, who were questioning accepted moral and political ideas.
The truth is that it was only later that teenage power began to emerge.
True, many young people challenged whether what their parents said
was right or good for them. By the 1960s young people became more
affluent and were not so dependent on their parents. This, together
with increasing exposure to the media, led to an independence of ideas.
From 1954 to 1968 the student population of most major countries had
doubled.

Roszak describes the move to a greater sense of self-determination:

Colin MacInnes (1967, pp. 567–89) discussing the difference between
youthful radicals of the thirties and the sixties, observes that the contemporary young 'hold themselves more personally responsible than the young
used to. Not in the sense of their 'duties' to the state or even society but to
themselves. I think they examine themselves more closely and their motives
and their own behavior' . . . their dogged pursuit of a directness and immediacy free of organizational-hierarchical distinctions. And yet it is, at worst,
the exaggeration of a virtue to insist that neither theory nor rhetoric must
submerge the living reality of our actions as they affect others and ourselves, to insist that the final appeal must be to the person, never to the
doctrine.

But then the question arises: what is the person? What, most essentially, is this elusive, often erratic human something which underlies social systems and ideologies, and which now must serve as the ultimate point of moral reference? No sooner does one raise the question than the politics of the social system yields to what Timothy Leary has called 'the politics of the nervous system' . . . For even in its most hostile caricatures, the bohemian fringe of our youth culture makes its distinctive character apparent. It is grounded in an intensive examination of the self, of the buried wealth of personal consciousness. The stereotypic beatnik or hippy, dropped out and self-absorbed, sunk in a narcotic stupor or lost in ecstatic contemplation . . . what lies behind these popular images but the reality of a sometimes zany, sometimes hopelessly inadequate search for the truth of the person? (Roszak, 1971, pp. 61–3)

It is my belief that 'sex and drugs and rock 'n' roll' were the means to break free from the oppression that many of that generation felt to be so diminishing. There was a wave of reaction to the implicit statement 'we know what's best for you'. It was this same conviction that the self, the person, was of supreme importance that inspired the humanistic movement. The aim of humanistic therapy was not to make people better citizens or to be 'normal' but to help them be themselves and to trust their experience.

This change was clearly reflected in the sphere of what was commonly regarded as mental health. There had always been great fear about insanity. Due to the work of Freud, particularly after his visit to New York in 1937, there was increased interest in the workings of the mind, which was reflected in novels and films of the 1950s focusing on the characters' inner turmoil, but it was still uncommon for people to admit to being in therapy. The popular image was of a mysterious process called 'analysis' for the well-to-do. For the rest, mental hospitals were the place they would be sent if they showed abnormal psychological behaviour. The grounds on which people were locked up for most of their lives were highly doubtful. For instance, in many Western countries single mothers were put into mental institutions for much of their lives. Many people who did not behave normally were locked up without a trial in what were called euphemistically lunatic asylums. Thomas Szasz (1972) in his book *The Myth of Mental Illness* challenged the right of psychiatrists to incarcerate people for being different or, in totalitarian regimes, to use psychiatry to impose political conformity through brainwashing. David Stafford-Clark (1952), a celebrated psychiatrist, author and broadcaster described in graphic detail the conditions that applied until the late nineteenth century in asylums.

It may seem beyond belief that physicians could contemplate other human beings naked, cold, crusted in their own excrement, chained and starving in the dark on stone floors, without pity and without remorse. But they could and they did, and it is only by the exertions and the example of exceptional men that our own standards have been raised above this appalling state. (Stafford-Clark, 1952, pp. 44–5)

The tendency to treat mental illness by purely physical methods was understandable when there was little else. In 1949 there were 150,000 people in mental hospitals in England. It is salutary that, not so long ago, ECT and pre-frontal lobotomy were heralded as breakthroughs in the treatment of depression and schizophrenia, followed by the widespread use of psychiatric drugs. This is not to dismiss these well-intentioned methods for relieving suffering, but they reflect a limited understanding of the human condition and emotions. Sadly they had questionable success with attendant risks and harmful side effects. Now we are faced with the advent of Prozac and its derivatives, which no doubt have relieved depression in many cases but have largely failed to address the original problems.

The humanistic movement was not just a rebellion against accepted norms and the ways of dealing with people with emotional problems – it was a new understanding of the human condition; one that was based on a positive view of people. There was an outburst of new ideas, methods and approaches that laid the emphasis on growth rather than cure. It questioned the concept of mental illness and the medical treatment of emotional disturbance. The psychiatric approach was inevitably based on dealing with people from the outside. Psychoanalysis was too focused on the inside. Humanistic psychology saw a fusion between what was happening inside a person and how he behaved. There was an acceptance of people as they are, a turning away from labelling people who are troubled. The scene was set for a radical change in the way people who were 'different' were treated. The dignity of everyone was being recognized, not merely in principle but in practice. And so the humanistic movement was born in an ethos of social and moral ferment.

This reaction to authority was a personal, moral, social and political rebellion. It affected almost every sector of human endeavour. There was a move away from authoritative methods in the field of education including training. There was a shift from deductive to inductive learning – learning through experience – a recognition that didactic methods were of only limited use in factual matters and that facts are more likely to be internalized as they become relevant for children and young people. Carl Rogers was teaching and practising the person-centred approach in education as well as counselling. AS Neill was pioneering an open form of learning at his Summerhill School. In the field of community development and youth work in Britain, the non-directive approach was being pioneered. An outstanding pair of teachers Dr Reg Batten and his wife Madge (1967) at the University of London Institute of Education had devised a method based on their community development work in Africa, which started from where people are. The youth service in Britain was affected by his approach and David Manship (1967) of the General Synod Board of Education, together with many others, influenced the whole field of training.

In the last resort there has to be a choice between an approach to know-ledge which tends to dull and imprison the inquirer and one which tends to stimulate and liberate him. The first choice entails the use of an uncriti-cally adopted theory or creed as a basis for a doctrinaire approach to life in which real experience, real needs and real situations become subservient to the promotion of an ideology. People become enslaved to an '-ism'. (If it is a good '-ism' it may take some time for people to recognize that the condi-tion is one of slavery rather than freedom.) The type of knowledge produced will tend to be blinkered and prejudicial, unrelated to experience (except by coincidence), and unproductive in the sense of being a clinical unfolding of what is already 'known' in principle rather than an adventure in new discovery. (Manship, 1967, p. 5)

Openness, authenticity, putting people first, trusting self, the move from accepting a given authority to what Ronnie Laing (1967), a famous radical Scottish psychiatrist, called 'the politics of experience' – these were the hallmarks of the alternative movement that were reflected in the person-al growth movement.

The outcome of this ferment was the establishment of three significant bodies: the National Training Laboratory at Bethel Connecticut in 1946, the Growth Centre at Esalen, California in 1961, and the Association of Humanistic Psychology, which was established at a conference at Old Saybrook, Massachusetts, in 1962. Although these were the visible centres of activity, they both inspired and brought together a large number of individuals and groups that were expounding and practising psycho-logical theories and therapeutic methods that were a radical alternative to those of the analytical schools – the behavioural and the psychiatric fra-ternity that had been generally accepted by the medical establishment for the previous 50 years as the bases of treatment. They came up with new models of personality and more optimistic views of the human condition, which were encapsulated in the saying attributed to Fritz Perls: 'you don't have to be sick to get better'. They were less concerned about the past than with gaining awareness in the present, seeing the client as the expert on her own life, rather than the therapist.

Chapter 2
Significant figures – the first generation

The next few pages describe a number of the leading figures who had a profound effect on the way in which psychotherapy was regarded and carried out and were the first generation of humanistic psychotherapy.

Jacob Moreno (1889–1974)

Romanian by birth, Moreno was educated in Vienna, where he met Freud but rejected the basis of his methods. As early as 1910 he started the Theatre of Spontaneity where people acted out their deepest feelings to regain a sense of themselves. When he moved to America in 1925 his theories were already well developed. There he found greater acceptance of his methods. By the 1930s he had established his own centre outside New York where he treated his patients through the use of psychodrama. His approach, which involved putting the client at the centre of the re-enactment of trauma, was clearly humanistic. His techniques for acting through critical situations became the basis of much of the group-centred therapy of the 1960s and 1970s in California. He emphasized the creative and spontaneous ability of people to resolve their personal and social problems. He used dramatic methods, which were highly active, to allow his patients to experiment with alternative ways of behaving based on the release (catharsis) of bound-up feelings:

> If the nineteenth century looked for the lowest common denominator of mankind, the unconscious, the twentieth century discovered or rediscovered its highest common denominator – spontaneity and creativity. (Moreno, 1934)

It was not until 1962 that the leading figures who pioneered what was called the 'growth movement' and were operating in different areas came together as an identifiable group. It was called the human potential movement and it is still recognizable as both a worldwide community and a powerful influence in many areas of life as well as that of personal development.

Abraham Maslow (1908–70)

Maslow was the outstanding figure in this movement and is regarded as the father of humanistic psychology. He was a teacher of psychology at Brandeis University where, in the 1950s, he identified from his research that there were certain common characteristics in people who experienced fulfilment in their lives, among which was self-acceptance, self-awareness and an inner directed sense of themselves. He coined the phrase the 'self-actualized person' in his most influential work (Maslow, 1962). This cut across the medical idea of mental illness, which was based on what he considered a false concept of normality. The main flow of his thinking was that people have a tendency for growth that represented a liberation from the fatalism in analytical therapy and a predisposition towards treating neurosis in psychiatry. There was a growing awareness of another model for human beings, which had a completely different emphasis. He believed that everyone has potential for change and growth. He concluded that human nature is capable of achieving the highest levels of experience, which he called transpersonal experiencing.

He did more to change our view of human nature than anyone in the twentieth century since Freud. Unlike the other figures, he was not a practising therapist, but his research, writings and activism inspired and galvanized almost everyone involved in the growth movement. After some years, he started the *Journal of Humanistic Psychology*. Together with some of the outstanding figures in psychological innovation, Maslow was the prime mover in the foundation of the Association of Humanistic Psychology in 1962 and later the Association of Transpersonal Psychology.

At the same time, new methods were being used to provide support and development for people who were either troubled by their lives or not coping with social norms, or were unhappy with the prescriptive culture of medical provision for emotional problems, and there was a move to change the way in which decisions were made in group and corporate life.

Kurt Lewin (1890–1947)

In the late 1940s and early 1950s, Kurt Lewin of Massachusetts Institute of Technology and his associates in the field of social psychology carried out a series of experiments on the east coast of the USA. At what became known as the National Training Laboratory (NTL) in Bethel, Maine, they set up unique learning structures, which they called T-groups (sensitivity training groups). These were based on Lewin's recognition of the need for human relations training in industry and commerce. They were very intense and challenging experiences. The purpose was to study the interaction between members, their own behaviour, and its effects on others. What developed from these courses was that those who attended identified the considerable benefits of a more participatory style of leadership. They discovered the power that people could find for themselves in the experience of the dynamic of small groups, where there was no leader in authority. It was a challenge to hierarchical forms of authority. It allowed the members of the training groups to discover the reality of shared leadership. Feedback was one of the primary tools. This concept was derived from the use of radar in receiving information back from a signal sent out. (Nowadays it is common for appraisals to include contributions from junior staff.) The expression of negative thoughts and feelings about what was happening in the group gave rise to an immense amount of knowledge about the 'process' in relationships (what was happening under the superficialities of organizational structures). It could be a long and laborious process but the results were effected much quicker as the resistance had already been worked through. For a thorough assessment of these early methods of encounter, see Bradford et al. (1964).

Carl Rogers (1902–87)

Probably the most influential person in the practice of humanistic psychotherapy was this quietly spoken, devout fatherly figure, whose roots were in Christian education and who studied theology at Union Seminary. In his belief that people are all right as they are, he rejected any idea of original sin. His approach to his clients was based on positive regard. He was a gentle man who treated people with respect and had no time for the faceless expert. He would say that anyone who wants to help someone to grow has to give up the idea that he knows what is best for his client. Through considerable research, he showed that people learn what they need to learn when they are trusted to discover for themselves.

At about the same time as the NTL experiments began, Carl Rogers introduced what became known as encounter groups in his practice in Chicago. His programme was designed to train counsellors to help veterans from the Second World War. This intensive experience was to help the personnel understand themselves better and this formed the basis of extensive summer workshops for many years. Like T-groups, the encounter groups were fairly unstructured and members set their own agenda. Whereas Lewin's primary aim was improved communication skills with a therapeutic spinoff, personal growth was the main emphasis of Rogers' groups. He was a man who reflected his beliefs about people in the way he lived. Marcia Karp of the Holwell Centre for Psychodrama, Devon, in a letter to *Self and Society*, recalls a memory of him.

> The most powerful image I have of working at the Institute was the day John Kennedy was assassinated. I heard the news in my psychology lecture with about 200 other students, all glued to transistors or radios. The shock was monumental . . . I stood up, in somewhat of a trance, and walked my

usual path to the Institute . . . When I got there, not a soul or sound was about. As if the place itself had died. I went from room to room, no one. Then I walked upstairs to Rogers' office; he was often in there working with the door open. There in his room were all the people I'd been looking for. There was silence. I walked in and sat on a chair amongst them.' No one spoke; a few were crying. Rogers was at his desk with his head down, cry-ing or sad, I wasn't sure. I felt at home. The room seemed to have its arms around me, around all of us. It was a place to feel my shock, not to deny it. No one asked me questions – one could just be there as a feeling person and it was all right – unconditional regard.

Bill Schutz (1921–2002)

On the west coast of the US, a number of radical leaders gathered around the growth centre called the Esalen Institute, which was established in 1961. This was the first of many growth centres that sprang up in the late 1960s and early 1970s. Esalen was the model but it had many advantages over its imitators. Many of the pioneers of the growth movement worked there regularly. It was a community and drew people from all over the world. It combined a commitment to personal freedom with strong influ-ences from Eastern philosophy. A new and distinctive approach to encounter groups grew up that was far more open than the basic encounter model of Rogers. Schutz encouraged people to be direct and to express their feelings honestly. In his workshops there was a great deal of physical expression including dance, fantasy and non-verbal contact. He was energetic in promoting greater freedom and excitement.

Fritz Perls (1893–1970)

Another one of the leaders at Esalen in the 1960s was Fritz Perls, a German analyst who originated a therapeutic method derived from gestalt psychology, psychodrama and Buddhism. He founded gestalt psychother-apy, theoretically based on the work of Max Wertheimer, Wolfgang Kohler and Kurt Koffka, which he studied before the war. Perls went to Vienna to train in psychoanalysis and was in analysis with Wilhelm Reich, a student of Freud. He left Europe and lived in South Africa during the war and was influenced by Jan Smuts' theory of holism.

In 1945 he moved to the USA, where he founded the New York Gestalt Institute in 1952. At about this time, he contributed to a major work with Paul Goodman and Ralph Hefferline: *Gestalt Therapy: Excitement and Growth in the Human Personality* (Perls, Hefferline and Goodman, 1951). The subtitle of this volume sums up his approach to working with people. He questioned the distinction between healthy and diseased con-sciousness (p. 448). He rejected psychoanalysis as mechanistic and

unholistic. He was undoubtedly the most charismatic and influential figure in the growth movement. A larger-than-life personality, he worked all
over North America, often in large groups, demonstrating his methods
using confrontation, catharsis and insisting that people face themselves
and the reality of the 'here and now'. He stressed the need to trust the
natural process:

> This type of organismic self-regulation is very important in therapy, because
> the emergent, unfinished situations will come to the surface. We don't have
> to dig: it's all there. And you might look upon this like this: that from with-
> in, some figure emerges, comes to the surface, and then goes into the
> outside world, reaches out for what we want, and comes back, assimilates
> and receives. Something else comes out, and again the same process
> repeats itself. (Perls, 1971, p. 23)

Each (human) organism acts as a whole. Health is the appropriate balance
and co-ordination of all that we *are*. At the same time he saw that self-
actualization was inborn and part of the change required is to get in
touch, through awareness, with the disowned parts of the personality and
move from environmental support to self-support. For much of this work
he used psychodrama and dreamwork. The difference from pure psychodrama and dream analysis was that he directed group members to be
the parts of themselves and their dreams, which he called dialoguing.
Although this was revolutionary in therapy, the implications were far more
radical. People were brought into acting their conflicts in their relationships, as Moreno had done, but they were also experiencing and
expressing their innermost thoughts and feelings in the present, rather
than talking about them.

He disliked the title 'psychotherapist'. He saw it either as a power trip
or a gimmick. The interaction of the culture of that period with the
growth movement was more obvious in California than anywhere else.
This was epitomized in the scene outside the hospital where Fritz Perls
died in 1970. Camped out on the grass for a week before he died was a
large group of young hippies. He had become a cult figure, looking more
like an eastern guru towards the end of his life. He was not only against
the establishment of psychotherapy but also against the government. He
refused to pay taxes for 10 years in protest against the war in Vietnam.

Although he is not a well-known player in the human potential movement, I think *Paul Goodman* (1911–72) is worth a mention here. A
colleague of Fritz Perls, and co-author of *Gestalt Therapy* (1951), he was
also a remarkable novelist, a writer on social affairs, and an anarchist in
the 1960s. His distinction was that he made an impact outside the world
of psychology in the fields of the arts, social affairs and commerce. For an
extensive account of his work, read Roszak (1971, pp. 178–204). He
embodied the alternative movement in seeing the possibility of a different
world order where humanistic principles could prevail.

Eric Berne (1910–70)

Another great innovator died in 1970. Although Perls and Berne met only once, together they produced two of the major methods of humanistic psychotherapy that are in use today. Berne was much more of an academic and his writings superseded the analytical conceptual framework with a completely new and pragmatic approach to therapy. Berne, who lived and worked for most of his life in and around San Francisco, was the most enigmatic of the leading figures who operated in California. Eric Berne was an undoubted genius who rebelled against the establishment after he was turned down for membership of the San Francisco Psychoanalytic Institute in 1956. In 1947, after leaving the army as a psychiatrist, he began working on his studies of intuition in which he rejected the Freudian concept of the unconscious. By the end of 1957 he had created a new approach to psychotherapy – transactional analysis (TA). The fruition of this work was the publication of *Transactional Analysis in Psychotherapy* in 1961.

He was a shy and secretive man with a brilliant wit and a down-to-earth sense of humour. He had the ability to make people chuckle as he revealed to them their hidden selves. He kept his personal life very separate from his public image. Many people found him distant and hard to get to know. In later years, he devoted himself increasingly to writing. The winter before he died he was working on six books. His weekly schedule was immensely demanding, although he always played poker on Friday nights. Although he was an eccentric and complex man who could be irritatingly argumentative, competitive and moody, it is clear that he took immense interest in other people's ideas and never failed to appreciate his patients for what he had learned from them. Without the personal magnetism of Fritz Perls, he drew a large number of followers who have since become leaders of their own brands of transactional analysis, including Claude Steiner, Jacqui Schiff and Bob Goulding.

Following the example of his father, who was a human and conscientious physician, he was devoted to his clients. He talked about therapists being 'real doctors', not purely in the medical sense, but practitioners who cured people. He had no time for the expression of negative feelings for its own sake and valued laughter as therapeutic. He was an iconoclast – the little boy who saw that the king wasn't wearing any clothes. He told a joke about the way that patients are diagnosed in the average clinic. 'The person who has less initiative than the therapist is called passive-dependent; the person who has more initiative than the therapist is called a sociopath.' He attacked the sham and put-downs in using a lot of big words and invented a system of therapy based on simple words that anyone can understand. In 1964 he published *Games People Play,* which became a best seller and launched transactional analysis into the realm of pop psychology.

Wilhelm Reich (1897–1957)

It is important to mention the important contribution of Reich, who was a pupil of Freud in Vienna. He not only developed psychoanalytical theory and practice but turned his thinking to psychological defensive mechanisms and how these related to the way the body functioned. 'Body armour' is the muscular defence built up to protect a person from prohibited feelings and impulses. He encountered strong opposition from some psychoanalysts for his insistence on the political significance of sex. He later described his decision to leave Vienna with some reluctance.

> The pressure exerted from every direction on this social hygiene work became so strong that I decided to move to Germany. In September 1930, I gave up my flourishing medical practice and psychoanalytical teaching in Vienna and went to Berlin. I went back to Austria only one other time in April 1933. During this brief stay I was able to address a large gathering of students at the University of Vienna. I outlined to them some of my conclusions in my work on the nature of fascism. As a psychiatrist and biologist, I considered the German catastrophe the result of a situation in which masses of human beings who had become biologically helpless had fallen under the sway of a few power-hungry bandits. I was grateful for the understanding which the student youth of Vienna offered me at that time. But there was not a single professional politician who deigned to listen. (Reich, 1951)

His last years were spent in the USA in the service of the Orgone Institute, which he founded. He developed some unorthodox medical ideas from his theory of 'orgone energy' and was prosecuted by the American Food and Drug Administration for fraud. He died while undergoing imprisonment for contempt of court.

He was a revolutionary figure in his own right but also had a considerable effect on many of the prime movers of the growth movement in Europe and the USA. Both Perls and Schutz at Esalen used his body-oriented ideas and techniques, but it was his student, Alexander Lowen, who developed his theories into bioenergetic therapy, which has contributed to an understanding in therapy of how emotions are seated in physical symptoms which can be unblocked by techniques which open up the system. His famous saying was that 'the body doesn't lie'. Energy, according to Reich, is inhibited through painful experience and is trapped in the body and becomes a person's character structure, through which he expresses himself and his neurosis. Another psychotherapist, Joseph Cassius integrated bioenergetics into the theory and practice of transactional analysis, which he called body scripts. Dozens of other body therapies owe their origins to Reich and these represent a whole field of humanistic psychotherapy.

Ronnie Laing (1927–89)

Alongside the humanistic developments in the USA, there was the *existential* movement in Europe. This originated with the philosophy of Dostoyevsky and Kierkegaard in the nineteenth century, Sartre and Buber in the mid-twentieth century and developed into the existential psychology of Laing and Frankl (1959) who, together with Rollo May and Irvin Yalom in the USA, form the main contributors to this approach to therapy. There has always been a close relationship between existential and humanistic psychology. Indeed May, together with James Bugental, another leading existential thinker, was a member of the founding group of the American Association of Humanistic Psychology. There are some overlapping beliefs and practices: the 'I–thou' nature in the therapeutic relationship; the need for the therapist to be open and authentic; the emphasis on self-awareness; together with the twin realities of freedom and personal responsibility.

Laing was very much his own man – highly charismatic, he lectured to large audiences on both sides of the Atlantic. Although he was a brilliant thinker and writer in his own right, he was also man of deep compassion for people. He denounced the natural scientific approach of Freud and called for a science of persons. In spite of his own background and training as a psychiatrist and as a psychoanalyst, he attacked these accepted theories and practices as not sufficiently grounded in human experience. He became labelled as an anti-psychiatrist. In fact he was not against psychiatry per se but he was opposed to the way in which it was used in denying freedom and the realities of internal perception, and the way it categorized people rather than listening to them. In 1965, together with colleagues and friends, he set up the Philadelphia Association, which is still in existence. It had a number of households devoted to providing a safe haven for people to go through psychotic breakdown without the dehumanizing effect of psychiatric institutions. This experiment allowed people to discover their own inner truth and go mad without the interference of involuntary treatment and diagnosis. Their alienation is to make their own sense of the insanity around them. To provide an environment in which they can find a creative way of discovering a more authentic way of being. There was a harrowing play based on his work there called *Mary Barnes* (Edgar, 1979) based on one of his clients at the Philadelphia Association, which illustrated his methods of allowing people to have their madness and working through it.

It is hard to put Laing into a category. Clearly he saw himself as an existialist and that is the main thrust of his writing. Certainly he was a central figure in the humanistic movement and believed in living life to the full. He died playing tennis. His last words were 'Is there a doctor in the house?' An affectionate tribute to his life and work was compiled for television, shortly before his death called *Did you used to be Ronnie Laing?* which exposed his humanity.

Other significant figures

Alongside these leading thinkers and practitioners who made such a big impact in the late 1950s and 1960s were a number of other important innovators, leaders and writers who made a substantial contribution, who shared in this process of change in thinking and practice, and were a major part of the alternative movement. There are too many to mention them all but here are a few who have left a distinctive mark in the humanistic enterprise.

Roberto Assagioli was an Italian psychiatrist who was influenced by Jung in making analysis about what is the spiritual self as well as the unconscious self of Freud. He posited that the self had a number of parts and concentrated on a method of structured fantasy to help people get in touch with the various parts of themselves (sub-personalities). So, like Jung, he was concerned with the higher self, the part that can acquire wisdom and insight from within. He was involved in the beginnings of the humanistic movement in the USA and represented the aspect of humanistic psychology that emphasizes the spiritual aspirations of people. Personally I think his most telling book was entitled *The Act of Will* (1984) in which he gave a place for self-discipline in the process of change.

Sidney Jourard was a professor of psychology at the University of Florida and sought to establish that the truth about ourselves is real only when we are open with others. One of the shifts in humanistic psychology was that the most effective way of increasing a sense of personal power is experienced through developing awareness and skills in relationships; hence the proliferation of groups. Individual therapy is limited to a relationship of two in which the change is based on the quality of the relationship. Jourard (1971) worked on the principle of self-disclosure and did some significant research to show in various settings how more effective and healthy people could be by being more transparent – taking themselves out of roles and showing themselves to be much more than they appear when hiding their feelings.

Bill Swartley was an active member of the human potential movement in the USA who brought together regressive techniques with the principle of self-regulation and an open style of facilitation to cathect early trauma. As the encounter movement put most of its eggs in the basket of experience, so Swartley extended this to the experience of pre-natal life. This forms a neat bridge between the Freudian 'unconscious' and Perls' 'here and now'. In fact much of Swartley's approach was influenced by Perls' stress on taking responsibility for self. At about the same time, in the UK, *Frank Lake* (1915–82) was developing clinical theology, based, like Swartley's approach, on LSD experiences that regressed people back to birth experiences. For a time, both called their approach 'primal integration', which was quite distinct from Arthur Janov's primal therapy. Just before his death in 1979 he started a programme of training in the UK and this has been carried on by Richard Mowbray and Juliana Brown at the Open Centre, and by others, including John Rowan.

Ivan Illich is not a well-known name, although he wrote a number of books questioning established systems of education, medicine and religion. He was a man who lived his ideals. He grew up in Vienna of a Croatian father and Jewish mother. He was ordained a Catholic priest and by the age of 29 he was a Monsignor. He worked in the Puerto Rican community of New York and later was in constant conflict with the Church over his radical views. After some fierce antagonism from the Vatican in 1968, he left the priesthood and devoted himself to lecturing, writing and campaigning for humanistic causes. He was courageous in applying his brilliant intellect to political and social issues. He set out to break down ideologies that were dehumanizing. *Celebration of Awareness: A Call for Institutional Revolution* (1971) was the appropriate title of one of his books.

Summary

What was it that united such a disparate and individualistic group of thinkers and their models of therapy? What brought about the confluence of this wave of alternative approaches was that they *were* alternative. They shared a suspicion of the establishment of psychotherapy – both the medical model and analytical anonymity. Also, to a greater or lesser extent, perhaps it was their openness – not being dogmatic, avoiding making exclusive demands for the truth. They involved people in the process of their own therapy. At the same time the work of these pioneers carried a strong social implication for the way in which people and groups related to one another outside the therapeutic environment. They had a deep discontent for the way in which people were manipulated for political and commercial purposes.

The burgeoning of *group work* was the main impetus to this development, which will be discussed further in the next section. In this kind of setting, which was very different from analytical groups, the participants could see for themselves what was going on between the leader and the members. The groups were interactional and both the leaders and the members were open to each other. Although many of these were highly confrontational in style, they were mostly carried out by therapists, who were willing to be open. This was not altogether true as some of them were highly charismatic and caused another kind of dependency and conformity. It was true that some of the leaders used their power in a way that would be questioned today. It has been said that many of the pioneers who pushed back the frontiers of human experience would not be accepted as members of the professional agencies that have been set up to further their work. Many of them were highly unorthodox and, in their own time, quite startling. Since the 1970s these therapeutic behaviours have been widely used and it is hard to realize today that psychotherapists making bodily contact, expressing strong feelings and sexual feelings and making a lot of noise was regarded in the late 1950s and early 1960s as unusual. It is important to stress that, although a lot of strange things went on in the early stages of the growth movement, most of these activities have now been regulated by professional bodies. And yet the enthusiasm may have been abated by the constraints not only of common sense but also the limitations imposed by misguided correctness. It is questionable whether the self-imposed constraints on emotional expression have been in the best interests of the clients.

Chapter 3
Groups

The spread of groups as a primary method of personal growth and therapy characterized the humanistic movement. By the late 1960s there was a bewildering array of groups of all sorts. In the USA, and later in Europe, the phenomenon of groups was the hallmark of the growth movement and for many years they were an inseparable part of humanistic practice. They embodied the break with established forms of therapy and provided an environment for personal freedom.

> The encounter movement exists largely outside the traditional help-giving institutions of society. Its strong egalitarian and anti-intellectual overtones may represent a reaction against many of the traditional institutional forms of help-giving and the dependence on the professional help-giver. Yet there is nothing new in the idea of using groups to make life better. Since time began small groups have flourished as healing agents whenever old values and behavior patterns were no longer working, and people were forced to question life and look at it anew . . .
>
> Despite their varied form and function, encounter groups do share common features. They attempt to provide an intensive, high contact, group experience; they are generally small enough (six to twenty members) to permit considerable face-to-face interaction; they focus on the here-and-now (the behavior of the members as it unfolds in the group); they encourage openness, honesty, interpersonal confrontation, self-disclosure, and strong emotional expression. The participant is usually not labeled a 'patient' and the experience is not ordinarily labeled 'therapy', though the groups strive to increase self and social awareness and to change behavior. The specific goals of the groups may vary from reducing juvenile delinquency to reducing weight. Occasionally they seek only to entertain, to 'turn-on', to give experience in joy, but generally the overall goals involve some type of personal change – change of behavior, of attitudes, of values, of life-style. (Lieberman, Yalom and Miles, 1973, p. 4)

Since the 1960s, there has been an enormous growth in the development of groups and in the range of their application. Broadly speaking, this has fallen into three main streams – training, personal growth, and therapy. Shaffer and Galinsky (1974) identified 11 different types of group culture:

- the social work group;
- the psychoanalytic therapy group;
- the dynamic therapy group;
- the existential-experiential group;
- psychodrama;
- the gestalt therapy workshop;
- behaviour therapy in groups;
- the Tavistock approach to groups;
- T-groups and the laboratory method;
- the encounter group; and
- the theme-centred interactional group.

Shaffer and Galinsky (1974) is a classic work on groups in which the authors describe their history, ethos, key concepts and working assumptions, including the role of the leader. It is enjoyable to read and shows the diversity of group therapy very clearly.

Psychoanalytic groups have been used for decades. Originally the analyst treated the group as the patient and emphasized transference and resistance by interpreting the behaviour of the group without identifying anyone or being involved or revealing anything about himself. Although some of these groups were influenced by the growth movement, and the facilitator became more personally open, there was a clear distinction between these early groups and growth groups both in the style of leadership and the central feature of growth groups, which was based on experience and self-awareness. Growth groups avoided the analytical approach based on the interpretation of the consultant. They allowed members to explore their own needs or problems. Most of the early experimenters with growth groups avoided the term 'therapy' to distinguish them from the medical model of diagnosis and treatment.

Parallel to this was the increasing use of group work methods in the world of industry and commerce. It became fashionable to run management training based on the models of T-groups or encounter groups. They were seen as a new technology for change. The training programmes had a number of characteristics in common:

First, they were designed so that learning took place primarily in small groups, allowing a high level of participation, involvement, and free communications;

Second, they were all to some extent or another 'process' as distinct from 'content' orientated. That is, the primary stress was on the feeling level of communications, rather than solely on the information or conceptual level;

Third, they were all orientated towards improving the human relations or social skills of managers as distinct from their task or technical skills.

The means they used to achieve some of these objectives were, however, very different, notably on some of the following dimensions: degree of structure of the experience, directiveness of trainer, balance of 'content'

and 'process', level of inter-personal intimacy, degree of participant choice
of learning tools, person versus group-centred orientations, etc. Some of
the programmes were known to have a high degree of structure through
pre-planned time-linked exercises while others were known to be relatively unstructured with a high degree of participative learning. (Cary L Cooper
and David Bowles, 1977, p. 3)

This, then, constitutes the *first* application of group work to training.
From these origins in the T-group and the Tavistock model there were
numerous applications of group learning in the fields of social work, education and management, which are still used today. The T-group leader
tended not to participate but to leave the members to explore their own
individual processes and to become aware of their part in the group's
dynamics as it happened in the here and now. Bion's work on group
behaviour derived from a psychoanalytical background, with greater focus
on individual behaviour. Under the leadership of AK Rice this approach
formed the foundation of the Tavistock Conference, lasting two weeks,
which concentrated on interpersonal and inter-group relations. It
employed Bion's theoretical model of what happens in groups, incorpor-
ating some of the characteristics of the T-Group model. Apart from the
T-group model, which was the prototype growth group, there are a number of types of humanistic groups that have been applied to both personal
development and psychotherapy.

The *second* and most distinctive purpose of groups was that of personal enhancement embodied in the encounter movement, which broke
normally accepted boundaries of behaviour. The basic encounter
approach of Rogers encouraged transparency and emotional openness.
The open encounter groups devised by Schutz represented the spirit of the
age even more. He and those who emulated his work actively encouraged
people to find a higher potential for celebrating life by providing structures to liberate people's hidden feelings in the here and now. These were
experiential groups that were no doubt influenced by the prevalence of a
hippy culture in California. Encounter groups were highly emotional experiences, both individually and between members of the groups.

The characteristics of encounter-type groups are freedom to discover
self, being open and honest with the group, self-disclosure, expression of
feelings, giving feedback, learning through experience, support and confrontation by group members, as well as gaining a sense of personal
power. Some encounter groups were motivated by the leader's charisma,
or the leader chose at times to structure the group with exercises or fantasies. The style of the group leader could be directive, supportive, or
confrontational, aiming at catharsis and body awareness. Some group
leaders might step out of their roles and become participants. Others
would be more concerned with enabling the members to make their own
decisions. The group could be a place where the expression of feelings
was encouraged and the emphasis was on the freedom for people to be

themselves and to avoid pretence and roles. A variety of group exercises were used to assist members to develop self-awareness and group sensitivity. Some groups began to feel a sense of their own power and challenged the authority of the leader, just as the original leaders had challenged the rules about the way people could behave in groups. Some rebelled against the leader and managed without.

Although most of this was fulfilling and liberating, there was, and maybe still is, a tendency for both leaders and members to try to enforce the standards of the group on everyone through confrontation and intolerance of phoniness. This can become a plague where anything that doesn't fall within these parameters can be a target of persecution, forcing people to use certain words or never being permitted to talk indirectly about something or someone. All of which has the well-meaning intention of helping a person to be straight and avoid role-playing but can become indoctrinating rather than liberating. Much of the activity that goes on in groups is supportive but people who come into this environment for the first time can find it shocking.

Lieberman, Yalom and Miles (1973, p. 424) studied 14 encounter groups representing 10 approaches. These approaches cover a wide range of widely differing group experiences but all share some of the core values described above. The approaches studied were:

- national training laboratory (T-group);
- Synanon;
- gestalt therapy;
- psychodrama;
- transactional analysis (TA);
- marathon;
- Esalen eclectic;
- psychodynamically orientated;
- personal growth (Western style);
- leaderless groups (encounter tapes).

They assessed the leadership behaviour patterns and their impact, the group norms and conditions, their effects and outcomes, and their ability to maintain change. They sought to test a list of 'myths' that outlined the popular views of the time:

- feeling, not thought;
- stay with the 'here and now';
- let it all hang out;
- there is no group, only people;
- feedback is the core experience;
- encounter groups are safe;
- 'getting out the anger' is essential;
- enthusiasm equals change;

- you may not know what you've learned now, but when you put it all together . . .;
- it all washes out when you leave the group.

It was clear from their findings that none of these beliefs went far, although they contained a limited measure of truth. Moreover, no type of technique or leader showed a high yield in outcomes. There were other less-tangible factors at work: the composition of the group, the flexibility of boundaries, intuitive psycho-sociological factors. A third of participants showed some useful effects a year after the groups. At least the groups provided a setting, albeit temporary, which enabled them to engage with others in a way that is unavailable elsewhere

There were casualties as a result of the intensity of these experiences where normal external restraints were left outside and where many of these groups attracted some people who were unstable. During my first experiences in groups, I noticed that some participants became quite disturbed. I remember one woman wandering about, talking incoherently. Another man ended up in a psychiatric hospital and his family brought a complaint against the organizers of the workshop.

The *third* strand of group work was that of psychotherapy. This seemed to have the clearer objective of providing a safe place for people to resolve their life issues. Some of these were problem centred, some were more process orientated, and some were more structured forms of stimulating growth through creative and physical expression. They tended to draw elements of the various group-work models and apply them to their own particular form of therapy whether it was transactional analysis, psychosynthesis, bioenergetics, primal, art or drama therapy. By the early 1970s the open group was the prevalent force in the humanistic movement. The leading methods of humanistic therapy all had their own particular modes in the use of groups. Most used groups, almost to the exclusion of individual sessions. Over the past 10 years this trend seems to have reverted and most humanistic therapists do more individual work than work in groups. It is sad to reflect that there are very few encounter group experiences available these days.

It is hard to overestimate the place of groups in the human potential movement and in humanistic psychotherapy. Apart from the contribution of encounter groups one must not forget the primary role that the techniques and philosophy of Moreno's psychodrama occupies. He introduced movement and action into group work and showed his successors the way forward. Fritz Perls used psychodrama methods and adapted them for his particular brand of dialoguing. Unlike the other group methods, he tended to work with people individualistically sometimes in large groups, which were like a Greek chorus. Eric Berne originated transactional analysis as a group method. It was in this setting that the 'games people play' were acted out and made accessible.

The boom in groups included a wide range of emphasis, experience and purpose – personal growth, therapy, training, supervision and professional development. There seemed to be a group for everything and anything. There are now counselling/peer groups for almost every aspect of the human condition – illness, addiction, trauma, gender, sexuality, families, abuse, and so forth, most of which have a therapeutic purpose.

There is not sufficient space here to expand any further on the dazzling array of group-based therapies in their many differing forms. I hope that it is enough to have demonstrated that group culture can be markedly variable. For further reading about the development of group work see Lieberman, Yalom and Miles (1973), Shaffer and Galinsky (1974), Rowan (2001), Bradford et al. (1964), Rogers (1970), Schutz (1967), Greenberg (1975) and Berne (1966).

Chapter 4
Developments – the second and third generations

The second generation represented a time of consolidation. By the early 1970s, there were institutes and centres combining training and therapy. There were also a number of publications that gained a place not only within the field of psychotherapy but in the popular market. It is fascinating to see the breadth and originality of many of the writings, training courses and therapeutic approaches that grew up during this period. Carl Rogers was the first to give the term 'counselling' a therapeutic application. Within 10 years this was increasingly being used as a way of dealing with all manner of people's needs. By 1968 the humanistic movement had two main centres – Bethel on the east coast of the USA and Esalen on the west coast. Within 10 years there were training institutes in the alternative therapies all over North America, and centres were being established in Europe.

The first growth centre in the UK was Quaesitor, founded in 1969 to promote the work of mainly US teachers in Britain. It is amazing to recall what went on there for the best part of 10 years. All the major approaches of the growth movement could be experienced there. In time, various training programmes were initiated and the early stages of the spread of humanistic methods in Britain emanated from here. The ideas and practices of alternative therapies were being taught to a wide range of people – mainly those in the helping professions and mostly through groups and workshops.

In Europe the ground was fertile for a change. The alternative movement was challenging the established relationships between men and women, parents and children in traditional family settings and between people in the workplace. This was due to the freedom given to own and express feelings, and awareness of the body as a storehouse of emotions.

It is worth noting a significant endeavour that was going on in South Africa. Influenced by the encounter movement, a group of people who had been trained in the USA returned to set up a programme of group work under the auspices of the Council of Churches to promote change and empowerment at the time when apartheid was dominant. Eoin and Joan O'Leary, Dale White and Colin Davidson were among them. As a result of their work there, a number of the leaders were deported and came to the UK to continue their humanistically based work in collaboration with the Churches in England.

In the same year that Quaesitor was set up, the Association of Humanistic Psychology (AHP) was founded by a group of British professionals who saw the need to promote humanistic thinking and practice internationally and in the following years promoted conferences in Europe and further afield, leading to the formation of the European Association of Humanistic Psychology in 1978. They continued to be at the cutting edge of humanistic development for nearly 20 years and, in co-operation with their partners in others countries, furthered the cause. Later, they became involved in political and social issues. John Rowan (2001) described his own experiences of this whole endeavour graphically.

From the standpoint of this present volume – the practice of psychotherapy – 1980 saw a radical move in the launch of the Association of Humanistic Psychology Practitioners (AHPP), a response to the need to set professional standards for humanistic practice in a wide range of fields. This was, and still is, a unique organization that does not exist elsewhere, bringing together practitioners from almost every humanistic discipline.

In the early 1970s, the Institute of Transactional Analysis (ITA) was founded by Dr Michael Reddy, who also launched the European Association of Transactional Analysis. Programmes of training in gestalt therapy were set up in London, Scotland and later in Italy by Isha Blumberg. The next few years saw the establishment of a number of humanistic centres offering programmes in alternative therapy, mainly in London – the Open Centre, which was set up by people who were involved in Quaesitor before it closed in 1977, the Churchill Centre, Spectrum, Community and others. The Boyesen Centre was founded at about this time, specializing in biodynamic massage. The Chiron Centre was established later by former trainees of Gerda Boyesen. Both of these are training agencies and therapy centres.

At the same time, various training courses were being organized, based on humanistic principles. With the closure of Quaesitor, David Blagdon Marks, who was its director, decided to embark on another endeavour. Together with some of the leading trainers from AHP and Quaesitor, he attempted to provide a recognized training in humanistic practice through the Institute of Human Potential, which ran a diploma course. Other diploma courses followed. The Institute of Psychotherapy and Social Studies (IPSS) started a programme to bring together the humanistic and analytical approaches. Some of those involved split and formed a psychotherapy training course on similar lines, which was later called the Minster Centre and was directed by Helen Davis. John Southgate set up a Diploma in Applied Behavioural Studies (DABS) at the North London Polytechnic, which was an open-ended method of learning about groups, relationships and attitudes to self. John Heron was responsible for the foundation of the Human Potential Research Programme at Guildford

University. At Whitelands College, Putney a group of trainers put on counselling courses based on the encounter group work and student-centred approach of Carl Rogers, which later developed into the Diploma in Humanistic Counselling at Roehampton Institute. John Andrew Miller pioneered the first MA course in humanistic psychology in Britain in 1977, sponsored by Antioch University in the USA. This was an outstanding example of a structure within which students could choose their own field of study from a foundation year that covered the spread of therapeutic approaches available.

One of the little-known pioneers in these early years was the Church of England Board of Education, which set up a programme of professional development under the influence of the Bethel T-group model in the early 1960s. Although it was parallel with the Tavistock Institute model pioneered by WR Bion, it had its own distinctive purpose, which was to awaken those occupying leadership roles to their feelings. Harold Wilson, who initiated this work, saw that much creativity and vision in the Church and other institutions was being stifled through repressed anger, which was seen as bad. In these institutes, as they were known, people began to find ways to express their feelings, which were so often trapped by moral, social, political or religious structures superimposed on them. Many of those who came were ordinary people from professional and commercial backgrounds who began to question the way in which authority was managed in their working situation as well as in their personal lives. The main feature was unstructured groups where there were minimal rules and the facilitator remained passive or reactive. This gave rise to a level of interpersonal communication not experienced previously. Participants learned that most decisions, plans, and interactions between people were based on emotions that were rarely expressed in the working environment. This in turn developed a freedom and a dilemma: how to maintain humanistic values within impersonal working establishments that not only included commerce and industry but also organizations with educational or social objectives. As a result of participating in the DABS course at the North London Polytechnic when I was training officer for the Board of Education, I wrote my dissertation entitled *Does it Work at Work?* in which I explored this conflict from my own experience. I came to the conclusion that this depended on three interrelated factors: a strong commitment derived from personal experience that the person-centred approach was the most effective and desirable in the workplace; support from colleagues and/or management and, lastly, a structure that was open to change. Sadly, but inevitably, this rarely happened. Either people went back and lost their vision or they left for a more attractive setting or occupation.

There was much criticism of 'group work' being responsible for breakdown in traditional family and hierarchical values. Latterly, however, there has been a gradual move towards a greater recognition of the relevance of personal and emotional issues in corporate life. Counselling and training groups are probably more prevalent than they were in the 1970s.

Although there were a lot of new developments, the reality was that these had a limited impact by 1980. This was largely due to the fact that there were comparatively few trained practitioners at this time. Apart from the handful of trainers, there were no clearly recognized standards and a number of transitory or new groups. This meant that, for a period, only a number of people were prepared to take the risk of entering into an experience that, although exciting, had an unclear self-authenticating standard. Often in the write-ups of workshops or groups, leaders would state that they had been trained by what they considered to be noteworthy teachers. Consequently it was a minority of people who had any idea what was on offer.

In the mid-1980s, however, humanistic therapy began to grow. The number of training agencies increased. A large number of professionals were turning to therapy as a career change or due to redundancy. Women whose children had grown up found a means of expressing their independence by taking up counselling and therapy. Self-employment, which was the norm in humanistic therapy, afforded an alternative working mode. The number of trainees on courses rose steadily through the late 1980s and early 1990s. In contrast with the general ethos of the Thatcher/Reagan era, which was more conservative and less alternative, many more people were seeking help through therapy. This was paradoxically due to the emphasis on the 'look out for yourself' motto that prevailed then. Politics was for the first time being aimed at meeting people's inner needs. This was portrayed graphically in the 2001 BBCTV series *The Century of the Self*. As a result of this self-betterment ethos, many more were turning to counselling and therapy to help their personal development with quite different motives from the earlier generation.

At a rough guess, the number of training agencies trebled in a 10-year period. Counselling courses accounted for a large proportion of these. Gradually, counselling was seen as a vital service to the community, especially in crises or emergencies. Specialist counselling services were being set up to deal with bereavement, crash victims, stress at work, cancer and, later, AIDS patients. More and more doctors' surgeries and hospitals were employing part-time counsellors. This trend showed a steep rise up to the mid-1990s, when the curve flattened out and trainers were beginning to have vacancies on their intakes. The agency that I worked for had 125 trainees on six courses in 1992. By 1997 the number had dropped to approximately 60 on two courses. Although the overall number of people seeking help through mainstream and alternative therapy was steadily increasing, the number of clients did not keep up with the number of graduates. Consequently newly trained therapists and counsellors found it harder to set up a viable practice. This in turn fed down the line to training. The boom in training had burst by the millennium. What we have at present is probably more realistic in terms of supply and demand. What I have described above applies not just to the humanistic sector but to the whole field of psychotherapy. This fact demonstrates another important trend in humanistic therapy: it is no longer seen as alternative and is self-consciously becoming more mainstream. This is not universally true. There was and still is a large minority of humanistic psychotherapists who regard themselves as part of the human potential movement and deplore their colleagues following the trend of respectability.

Recent developments – the third generation

We are now into the third generation in the growth of humanistic psychotherapy. During the 1990s there was a tendency for a large section of trainers and practitioners to shift their ground for both theoretical and practical reasons. It is noticeable that many of the pioneering schools have moved back (or forward, depending on your viewpoint) to analytical principles and have incorporated them into their teaching. It is not always clear what the reasons and motives for this have been. One possibility is to gain more social respectability; another could be a wish to be included by the medical/analytical system, which in the past was rejected by the humanistic movement. Another parallel shift has been the trend to gain academic respectability. This was clearly the case in the USA and in other parts of Europe much earlier. For many years in Britain there was only one master's degree available. Now there are at least 20 that are seen as qualifications in psychotherapy or counselling.

Then there are pragmatic reasons that could be seen to go alongside the theoretical change. Since the early 1980s there has been a change of sentience. Earlier, either due to circumstances or choice, humanistic practice had regarded itself as alternative, with the marks of rebellion, risk, experiment, and so forth. This was a badge with which many felt increasingly uncomfortable because, one can only assume, with more training becoming available, there was a need to compete with others in the field of therapy. With new people coming into the profession who had not been in on the alternative roots of humanistic therapy, the need to earn a living and to obtain employment began to take precedence over ideals. With this came the desire to gain acceptance in the more institutional realms of the health and social services. Consequently the humanistic field, with some exceptions, has set on a course to embrace the professional mainstream.

Now the reader may pick a note of criticism in this account but, although the writer would acknowledge this, the changes do not need to be regarded as a betrayal of humanistic principles. What it means is that some of the bases of growth movement have been eroded, such as the questioning of authority and the emphasis on experience over theory. In making a fair assessment of recent developments it is important to take into account three factors: the spread of humanistic principles beyond the humanistic community and indeed beyond the realms of therapy, and the higher level of competence and responsibility that generally applies to humanistic practice. Although there is something attractive about the free-spirited approach that was present in the early years, it has to be acknowledged that it would be only a small minority of folk who would go along with that now. Now, many clients come from more conservative backgrounds and do not necessarily wish to completely change their lifestyles and, for them, the more normative approaches presented by much of humanistic therapy seems to be more acceptable. Further elaboration of this theme will be found in Part Five.

Three important organizations in Britain have been founded that represent the change in this generation of humanistic and psychotherapeutic practice. As mentioned earlier, in 1980 the Association of Humanistic Psychology (AHP) saw the need to maintain high professional standards in humanistic practice. A number of their leading members formed the Association of Humanistic Psychology Practitioners (AHPP) – a body set up to accredit a wide range of practitioners, including therapists. There were about 20 categories having different requirements for membership. In 2000 this professional association became independent of AHP and called itself the UK Association of Humanistic Psychology Practitioners (UKAHPP) partly because this gave them a separate identity in relation to registration bodies, but also for accounting reasons, not to be limited to the charitable status of its originating body.

In 1980, the British Association for Counselling (BAC) was formed from a voluntary movement called the Standing Conference for the Advancement of Counselling. It became an independent body with its headquarters in Rugby. It had various sections, which were related to specialist areas of work. By 1985, it had introduced a form of accreditation for counsellors. This was, at the time, the only nationally accepted form of recognition. Many psychotherapists (as well as counsellors) from different disciplines became accredited by the BAC, whose membership grew appreciably over the years. Later, this body began to give accreditation to training courses that would give their graduates automatic membership. To my knowledge, a considerable number of agencies geared their training to enable their students to obtain this recognition, which gradually became the accepted standard for employing counsellors.

Aware of the success of this operation, the BAC saw the need for a similar approach in psychotherapy. In 1989 they sponsored what became known as the Rugby Conference, which brought together most of the organizations involved in the training of psychotherapists. This voluntarily based confederation was fuelled by the fear, when the European Union was established in 1992, that psychotherapists might not be able to practise legitimately without some form of registration. This fear turned out to be unfounded. Nevertheless, by the time that the EU was in place, the Standing Conference for Psychotherapy, as it had become known, had moved into becoming an umbrella organization and, in 1993, the UK Council for Psychotherapy was formed. It had the unique distinction of bringing together representatives from the whole range of psychotherapy training and accrediting bodies.

The Association of Humanistic Psychology Practitioners (UKAHPP) was one of the prime movers in the establishment of this national body as it saw the benefit of gaining greater recognition for its members and having 12 years experience of accrediting psychotherapists. It became a representative body within the Humanistic and Integrative Psychotherapy Section (HIPS), which occupies a large part of the national registering body for psychotherapy (UKCP). There were 24 training and accrediting organizations in this section represented on the Council. The other sections are:

- analytical psychology;
- behavioural and cognitive psychotherapy;
- experiential constructivist therapies;
- family, couples, sexual and systemic therapy;
- hypno-psychotherapy;
- psychoanalytic and psychodynamic therapy;
- psychoanalytically-based therapy with children.

This is an enormous advance from the days, not that long ago, when those who then called themselves 'alternative' were a minority and were regarded as 'fringe'. It would be true to say that not only has the humanistic movement grown, but also that it has influenced the world of psychotherapy and the helping professions. The insights and techniques of humanistic methods are now used in a wide range of education and developmental areas. There was a time, for example, when something as commonplace nowadays as role-play was viewed with great suspicion, even in a training context.

Although bringing together most forms of psychotherapy into one body is a remarkable achievement, many practitioners are opposed to it on the grounds that it represents a minority of psychotherapists; from a humanistic standpoint, individual therapists have no say and question the form of accreditation demanded for registration; they do not accept that statutory registration is a healthy direction for the practice of psychotherapy – it takes away its independence and it is seeking to corner the market by defining what should be regarded as a psychotherapist. Some of these banded together to form a loosely knit alternative organization called the Independent Therapists Network (ITN), which favoured peer and client assessment based on autonomous groups of therapists.

Despite this opposition, the UKCP has become a strong body with a number of committees set up to review a number of professional matters. Although there are clearly power issues at work, it has gained an increased standing outside the world of psychotherapy. Most of the humanistic agencies set up to train or accredit in humanistic methods are represented in this national body under the Humanistic and Integrative

Section (HIPS), including the UKAHPP, which is the only body that accredits psychotherapists as well as other practitioners under a number of categories across the range of humanistic practice.

The UKAHPP is also an accrediting body for registering those of its members who are counsellors in the parallel body recently been set up by the British Association for Counselling (BAC) – the UK Register for Counsellors (UKRC), which does not yet have a spread of representative bodies comparative to UKCP. The BAC, in turn, has extended its brief to include a new category of membership for psychotherapists. At the same time it has changed its name to British Association for Counselling and Psychotherapy (BACP). If you are not in the business you may be confused by the different bodies involved. Some of those within the field are confused as well!

How has this practical, social and philosophical change in humanistic practice affected the delivery of the service to the public? Directly, very little. Probably most people were only vaguely aware of the differences in the various types of therapy available. Although there has been more exposure in the press and media about the practice of psychotherapy, there has been little to educate the general public about the variety of approaches that are on offer. One series on Channel Four in 1986 entitled *A Change of Mind* made a bold attempt to expose the different forms of therapy. This had the merit of allowing viewers to see how these were practised, with a number of therapists talking through what they were doing with clients.

However, there have been two major developments that have helped indirectly to give a clearer basis for the profession. One is the setting of standards for training. It is now generally recognized that, in order to practise, a minimum period of four years part-time training is required. This includes a set number of hours for course work, supervision, personal therapy and field work. In the area of humanistic training this is very demanding and expensive. For a more detailed account of the requirements for training, see the UKCP Register available in public libraries. The drawback is that this is not universally accepted. For instance, there are a large number of competent therapists who were qualified prior to, or outside, the standards prescribed by the UKCP, or who have chosen for philosophical or political reasons not to join the registration track.

The second development has been a growing recognition of the need to protect the public by having an ethical framework within which psychotherapists are expected to practise. At the same time, complaints procedures have been set up by the training or accrediting agencies to enable clients to bring any matter in which they consider to have been unfairly or wrongfully treated by a practitioner. It is important that psychotherapists, humanistic or other, are accountable both to their clients and to some professional body.

The benefits of these developments are obvious. The deficits are not so clear. The negative effects are that so much control is involved that many practitioners have become overly careful in what they do for fear of reprisals. This could lead to a dampening of the creativity that is the essence of humanistic psychology. In the climate where there is a need to gain respectability, it might be that making things 'safe' has resulted in clients receiving a sanitized form of therapy. In humanistic training, it is important that trainees are regarded as partners in the learning process, just as therapists seek an equal relationship in the consulting room. I remember an eminent teacher saying that all therapists should experience some form of intensive encounter group as part of their training. The purpose of this is to enable people who work closely with others to have experienced an egalitarian form of emotional interaction based on energy rather than power. There are few trainers who are able to offer this, and it is questionable whether it would still be regarded as important enough to encourage trainees to seek it.

It is worthwhile to note that, since 1988, therapy and counselling have gone through an evolution and there has been widespread recognition of their value in a wide range of applications. There are far more people seeking therapy and a far greater number of therapists with a humanistic orientation, but it has to be said that the distinctive contribution from the humanistic movement is less obvious. This is a major reason for writing this book – to show the advantages of this approach and to encourage people to be more discerning in their choices, whether they be clients or people looking for help, trainees or those seeking training, psychotherapists, trainers, teachers or officials.

PART TWO
BELIEFS AND PRINCIPLES

Chapter 5
Humanistic beliefs

The practice of humanistic psychotherapy is based on a set of core beliefs about people and the principles and process involved in the therapeutic relationship. Humanistic beliefs and practices find expression in many ways and have been derived from a number of sources over centuries, including some primitive cultures, Greek philosophy, Christianity and other religions, together with the aspirations of the Reformation, the Renaissance and the Romantic movement. These coalesced in contemporary culture through the humanistic and the existential movement of the early 1960s. It is not the purpose of this book to expand on these derivations, as they are described at greater length in Schneider et al. (2001). My own view is that the true basis of these beliefs lies not so much in an idealistic picture of how people should be, but in a philosophy arising from experience. This is more than a purely pragmatic philosophy and seems to arise from what is worthwhile and purposeful in human nature. What humanistic psychology has done is to make these beliefs more visible and to use them as a basis for helping people to improve their sense of their humanity through a helping relationship.

Although most of society, including the world of humanistic therapy, accepts certain codes of conduct, humanistic psychology does not expound a right way of life. This belongs to realms of religion and politics. Although you would probably find some agreement among therapists about moral issues, they would not claim to know what is best for their clients. The objective is to help them to discover this for themselves. Even though humanistic therapists all have their own ideas, they avoid foisting them on the people who come to them, and help them to find their own truth.

While I was Chair of the Association of Humanistic Psychology Practitioners, a working party was set up to make a statement concerning what was considered to be the basis of the humanistic approach. Members were invited to contribute their ideas from their training and experience and, after a year of consultation, an agreed statement of core beliefs and practice was published in the 2000 handbook. I have drawn a lot from the thinking that went into this and its results in writing this section. Although I participated in this process, due recognition must be given to the work that was put into it by a number of people, particularly Christopher Coulson, who initiated the working party, and Tony Morris who brought together the final statement.

What follows may not necessarily represent the complete range of humanistic psychotherapies. Moreover, not all practitioners would accept all of the principles included here. Nevertheless, it aims to be a fair reflection of what are generally accepted as the basic tenets of the humanistic approach. One of the most important aspects of humanistic psychology is that it is inclusive rather than exclusive, taking a range of views and practices set out later in this book.

The central belief that motivates humanistic endeavours is that people come first. They are not parts of an organization. They are not units of human resource, as one prospectus for an educational institution described students. They are not votes. They are all individuals with their needs, rights, strengths and limitations. We have a string of words in our language that hide this essential truth – customers, patients, employees, managers, clients. To describe people like this is no doubt a convenient shorthand but it can easily cover the essential worth of every human being. John Kennedy was President when the first American was killed in Vietnam. He was deeply troubled by the fact that one man was dead under his administration. Some may say he should have cried for the thousands of Vietnamese who were already victims of war. We might have an absorbing debate about the comparative value of life when we are prepared to sacrifice so many in a 'just' cause. The fact remains that no matter how we justify cruelty, torture and death, the argument stops at the loss of loved ones. Now, obviously, we cannot run the enterprises of the world, particularly in times of emergency, to cater for every individual's need. But that is our aim – that is what a humanistic therapist seeks to do: treat everyone as though, at least for the time of contact with them, they are most important.

It would be a generalization, but one that is not far from the truth, to say that most of the problems that our clients bring to us are due to them not being treated as unique and of value at some vital time in their life. This is often because those who have the care of them have not seen them as persons but as the projection of their own problems or needs. What we seek to do is to provide a place where they can rediscover their own intrinsic worth.

What follows is an outline of humanistic psychology's fundamental beliefs about the nature of people, relationships and the environmental setting. These beliefs and principles are not limited to the practice of psychotherapy but apply to all aspects of human existence.

Every human being has essential worth

Everyone is 'born OK' with a tendency to do what is best and, given free-dom to choose, will prefer harmony and therefore will move constructively, both personally and socially. We are not born in sin. Although it is true that Christianity has influenced much of humanistic belief, the humanistic approach renounces the belief in original sin while accepting the truth implicit in the assertion that man was created in the image of God. As my theology teacher said, original sin is neither original nor sinful. The 'fall', he taught, was a fall upward for mankind – an open-ing up of humanity to a greater range of possibilities. From their experience of life, people choose their path based first on survival. All ani-mal behaviour, including that of human beings, has purpose. Rogers asserted from his vast experience and research that man is a trustworthy entity and can be trusted to move in constructive ways from the sense of his essential value. It is important, at this point, to contrast the difference between unconditional and conditional worth. There is a profound dif-ference between the intrinsic worth of our existence and any evaluation of our behaviour. Our being is unquestionable; our actions may not be. There is a fundamental contrast between being and doing. Much of the language and literature of humanistic psychology is about being. Whatever we do, every life has its own unique value. This belief under-writes all the therapeutic work in which we engage. Clients are helped to restore their belief in themselves as intrinsically worthwhile. Every action of the therapist is aimed to support this good sense of self.

People are neither good nor bad – there is potential for both in human beings

Generally speaking, given conducive circumstances, people will move towards what is good for themselves and others. This raises the question of the nature of what is commonly called 'evil'. We are faced, increasing-ly through the media, with a wide range of inhuman acts. Are these inhuman or do we have to include them in the definition of what is human? At the time of writing, the world is still reeling from the terrorist attack on the USA of 11 September 2001. The word 'evil' is being applied to those who committed this atrocity. What is good in this situation? Time alone will tell what is in the greatest good. This also raises the parallel question – what is good? Most of us in our daily lives do not encounter extreme forms of violence. Hence we are shocked, and the media fasten on to events that are shocking. It is not the purpose of this book to enter into a lengthy discussion of these issues – rather it aims simply to raise them. As a working hypothesis, good is any action which is for the well-being of people. The aim of humanistic psychology is to follow a path that is clearly for this end.

Humanistic psychology reacted to the fatalism of psychoanalysis, which regards human beings as at the mercy of primal forces. While not denying the power of these forces, the humanistic position is that there is a stronger tendency for people to choose what is best for them and those around them. They also have the power to change and move from a level of pure survival to more fulfilling levels of experience. Abraham Maslow's (1970) concept of self-actualization set out how it is possible for people to achieve their greatest potential. In this sense, there is a strong existential belief that people make whatever sense they can of the situation they find themselves in, at whatever age, and live their lives accordingly.

This shared belief is expressed in different ways by the humanistic disciplines. In transactional analysis, for example, there is the school of redecision therapy, which holds that we all make decisions in early childhood before we can think in an adult way. Based on their intuition, children make the best possible decision within the limitations of their perception of what is going on around them. These early decisions are changeable in adult life when an individual is ready to face the limitations of those decisions and make further emotional decisions based on adult reality. In gestalt therapy, there is the concept of the organic whole in everyone that has a sense of purpose. This can be discovered through awareness of what a person is doing in the present and by changing the present they can change the way they regard the past – taking responsibility for what they have done. Although primal integration uses the earliest possible experiences in life, back to the womb, its direction is that through the release of energy bound up in the early trauma people can gain release from their limitations by regression. Carl Rogers was the most positive in this respect. He stated that, whatever difficulties people experience, there is always a way for them to discover within themselves a better path. The role of the therapist is to assist this process of self-trust.

We all have the capacity to choose

In his book *Man's Search for Meaning,* Victor Frankl (1959) describes the suffering he shared with others at Dachau. He concluded that when all the familiar goals in life are taken away, what alone remains is the 'last of the human freedoms' – the ability to 'choose one's attitude in a given set of circumstances'. We are not purely the victims of genetics, family, environment or circumstances, even though we are strongly influenced by these factors. People make negative decisions as a result of inadequate parenting, not knowing better or by the way they distort reality based on their interpretations of their early experience.

In humanistic therapy, when these factors are identified and worked through, it is possible for people to widen their options for choice. They are capable of changing through self-realization and awareness. How this process of change can happen varies both within the therapeutic relationship and outside. Carl Whitaker (1989), the celebrated family therapist, said that the most reliable concept in therapy is the parenting role of the therapist. 'The purpose of our parenting is to allow the patient to be free to become more and more of himself' (p. 151). This is also true outside of therapy. Therapy, in its widest sense, is not limited to the activity called psychotherapy or counselling. People change as a result of their experience of relationships. When I was a youth worker, I witnessed many young people change as a result of their contact both with caring workers and their peers. The youth club was a setting in which young people could have a new and alternative experience, which could change their view of themselves and their outlook on life. Largely because it was voluntary, it opened up a new set of options of thought and behaviour. This is also true of many other settings such as schools, colleges, or leisure activities. Within a favourable context, including therapy, people can discover new ways of thinking and acting. We have the power to choose. Once we are aware of one or more options, we are free from the apparent impositions of others or ourselves.

People are responsible for themselves

This leads to another primary belief of humanistic psychology. During the course of our life, from the very beginning, things happen to us that are outside our control. To start with we do not choose to be born, nor do we decide to be the sex we are, nor do we choose our parents or the environment in which we grow up. There are many things that have happened since then that are not what we would have liked. Nevertheless, we do make decisions based on our experience. What we do with all these events and circumstances is down to each one of us. One of the challenges of humanistic psychotherapy is to take responsibility for our lives. Those who accept this are capable of maturity – of supporting themselves and meeting their needs. People may not feel responsible for themselves or take responsibility for what they do or think; their belief is that others or events are responsible; but in the last resort each individual is the only one who is. Everyone is the master of his or her destiny. When a person does not recognize this truth he manipulates the environment and blames others for what he does. This is characterized by helplessness and dependency, or by controlling, and gives rise to 'phoniness' and playing 'games'.

Taking responsibility for oneself is the only reality. However well or badly we are treated, whatever good or bad things take place in our lives, no one or nothing else can do this for us. Of course, we shall be influenced by what happens. How we respond to these happenings is up to us even though we may not want to recognize this truth. It is true that people feel, think and behave differently in the light of certain events. Some people cry in the face of tragedy, others do not. A lot of people recover from awful events in their life; some never seem to get over them.

What lies behind this belief is the fact that we are all unique, however similar we may seem. Nobody but me knows what goes on inside my skin. 'There's someone in my head and it's not me' was a line from a Pink Floyd number. This is a way we can experience life, avoiding taking responsibility for ourselves. But it's not true. I have to do what seems best to me with the experience I've had or am having, even though at times I want to shout out 'someone else do it for me!'

So we have the power to choose and we can choose not to take responsibility for ourselves. If we don't then we are left with finding someone or something else to take this on for us. This can involve a lot of work, which is unlikely to change anything. The basis, therefore, of humanistic psychotherapy is that, when we do take responsibility, we have greater personal power to deal with whatever befalls us.

People have the power to change and grow

'Every individual, every plant, every animal has only one inborn goal – to actualize itself as it is' (Perls, 1970, p. 33). Humans, like all life forms, have a basic instinct for survival. All activity has a purpose. This was set out by Abraham Maslow (1970) in his theory of a hierarchy of needs – from a basic need for sustenance and safety to the higher levels of belonging and creativity. Others would say that people move uniquely in response to what they perceive as their present need. Many within the humanistic field would assert that we are not limited by our needs. There is something in the human spirit that not only enables us to rise above our problems, but also to aspire to something better for ourselves. This is referred to as abundance motivation. 'You don't need to be sick to get better.' This belief is more than achieving our aspirations, fulfilling our potential or finding our dream. It is the essential nature of man from primitive times to develop. We can see this clearly in evolution and the great enterprises of man. In the individual realm we see people expand enormously in knowledge and become what their predecessors would never have thought possible.

In humanistic psychology, however, we are concerned primarily with the inner self rather than activity in the external world, which is only a limited indicator of a person's well-being. In short, we are interested in what people think and feel as a way of breaking through to something new or recovering what was lost somewhere in the past. It is our belief that people can and do change. The nature of that change is up to each individual to decide. Also, you will find, in different disciplines, differing understandings of what kind of change is possible and how that change can take place.

Human beings are whole entities within the totality of their environment

People can only be who they are in the context of the world in which they live. We are all a part of humanity, the natural and material world. There is a contradiction here. We came into the world alone and alone we shall return. Yet we cannot know who we are, separate from the experiences we have in relation to our family group, our relationships personally and generally, the nature of our material existence in society and the world as a whole. Man is a whole. He is a body, emotions, thoughts, sensations, aspirations, which constantly interact with each other. Within ourselves we have expressions of our physical self, our emotional self, our thinking self and our spiritual self, but there is a *whole* self that is more than the aggregate of the parts.

One of the clear demarcation lines in humanistic belief is not only whether there is any entity called 'spiritual' but also whether it is relevant to psychotherapy. John Rowan (1987) infers that this is a given: 'One of the characteristics of humanistic psychology, which distinguishes it very sharply from secular humanism, is that it has a place for the spiritual' (p. 7). He refers to Maslow's emphasis on peak experiences. 'In humanistic psychology we are very interested in studying this kind of phenomenon, and seeing how in some cases it can change a person's life.' At the same time there are many who take a purely phenomenological approach to human experience. Although they may not deny other people's spiritual experience, they would not attribute it to the transpersonal. There is danger here of an interpretation, which may come from a belief that is not demonstrable.

In making these statements, it is necessary to put into their proper context whatever beliefs humanistic practitioners hold. They are beliefs based on observable data. For instance, a spiritual dimension often enables people to transcend the material conditions of their lives. It is the role of the therapist to offer these views to his clients as a basis for their work together. It is also important, where relevant, to state these views clearly, while allowing the client the option of refuting them. It is these beliefs that motivate the humanistic approach to psychotherapy

The truth about the nature of human beings is multifaceted

Humanistic psychology allows for a diversity of views. It is not dogmatic. It covers a wide range of methods and disciplines. It is open and inclusive. People can be predictable but there is always a hidden element that defies definition. We are more than our brains, chemistry, biology, physiology. The truth about people is more than the sum of all the parts.

Psychology is not a precise science. Some would question whether it is accurate to call it scientific. Certainly, it has some scientific aspects, but like true science the 'facts' are always open to question. There is fuzzy logic and the shortest distance between two points is not always a straight line. There is a strong body of opinion that describes this as 'spiritual'. If that refers to what is not known or understood, then it leaves the door open for speculation or faith. Many human experiences are beyond the realm of the rational, pragmatic and purely objective perception.

The other important issue here is that each person's experience has its own truth and it is more liberating and comprehensible to value that. How human beings behave, function or change is a matter of interpretation. The only truth is the mind of the seer and often this has its own agenda. Humanistic practitioners seek to be open about their agenda – not making claims for being right about anyone, accepting people as they are, believing their story and treating them in their own language or currency. I have deliberately used the word 'approach' in the title of this book because that is what humanistic psychotherapy really is – an approach, a movement towards, a thesis that has an antithesis and, for the moment, a synthesis. As John Rowan (2001) puts it so eloquently in the new edition of *Ordinary Ecstasy,* the humanistic position is a paradox and a contradiction.

Chapter 6
The therapeutic relationship

The essence of the humanistic approach to psychotherapy is in the nature of the relationship between the therapist and the client. This is the vehicle of change. What happens, whether in or out of awareness, is central to the process. In fact, it is this process that causes some kind of shift in the client's attitude or feeling towards herself and others. Petrūska Clarkson (1995) states that research shows that the outcome of therapy is mainly dependent on the quality of the relationship, not the theory, techniques or orientation of the therapist (p. viii).

Of course, there *is* only a therapeutic relationship in the same way that there is only a marriage: one that is accepted by two people and implicitly or explicitly given recognition by societal groups. What happens after the contract, implicit or explicit, has been made depends on the kind of relationship that is formed. It is the nature of this alliance that counts. There are various ways to describe this. Rogers clearly stated that the basis of a therapeutic relationship is what he called 'client centred'. He set out the core conditions of empathy, unconditional positive regard and congruence, which are most likely to provide the right kind of climate that would enable the client to change. Perls emphasized in his work the 'I–thou' nature of the humanistic relationship, a phrase used by Martin Buber, an existential thinker. Here the emphasis is on the personal nature of therapy. (How can it be anything other than personal?)

Alongside this, the balance of power in humanistic work has shifted towards the client (the customer is always right!). In his controversial book, *Against Therapy* Jeffrey Masson attacks the abuse of power in therapy. Although he cites many instances of this (only a few pages are taken up with humanistic therapy) the main emphasis of humanistic therapy is on the empowerment of clients. Bob Goulding (1978) talked about the power as being in the patient. Eric Berne (1961) saw the therapeutic contract made by the client to be the valid area of intervention for the therapist. For Ronnie Laing it was co-presence. This means that the therapist is present in all aspects of his being, not holding himself back. John Southgate in his handbook *The Barefoot Psychoanalyst* (1989), based on the work of Karen Horney, sees the client as the worker and the therapist as the assistant in the client's work. For me, the person who spelt this out most clearly was Claude Steiner, the originator of social psychiatry in his book *The Other Side of Power* (1982).

This emphasis on equality is to help the client discover her own power. The relationship is central to the client finding her own authority in her life, not merely to enhance the quality of the therapeutic relationship. The therapist is there for the benefit of the client. Probably most therapists would go along with this in principle, but the humanistic therapist, in his regard for the client, stands on this basic principle by openly and specifically asking the client to define her problems, needs and actions. This need not preclude making suggestions, but the aim is to keep the client in charge of her life, and to demonstrate that, although the therapist cares about the person, it is not his business to direct her life. He can help her to identify and clarify her needs and problems but all the time the therapist is inviting, sometimes probing, to assist the client to be aware of what she wants in the therapy.

Now, of course, it is true that therapists will exercise some degree of control in the management of the sessions – this is to provide an adequate framework within which clients can do what is necessary to improve their life. At times, therapists will give directions to promote the changes the clients wish to make, but always allowing for their refusal, which then can result in material about what is going on in the therapeutic relationship. By doing this, therapists do not assume that they are superior but rather that they are in a role that enables clients to grow through their experience of attachment with the therapist. If therapists behave in such a way as to encourage what is good, to be supportive in pain and not to judge, clients will begin to have a better sense of themselves.

Within the schools that comprise the 'humanistic family', there are differences in the way that power is exercised by therapists. For example, in body therapy, psychodrama and gestalt therapy, there is a greater emphasis on directing the client due to the fact that the basis of these methods is the use of techniques in order to heighten clients' awareness or raise their energy. In the field of transactional analysis there is a value placed on the use of the Parent ego state, not only as a model of the missing parenting but also to enable the client's change with its threefold therapeutic attributions of potency, permission and protection. The interventions in these tend to be confrontational or cathartic. This is certainly true in encounter groups, where the therapist is likely to occupy centre stage for some of the time to inspire, direct or even pressure members into taking risks to experience the dormant parts of themselves. In the person-centred approach the interventions are more likely to be supportive and reflective. Clients are encouraged to take charge of the sessions as a way of experiencing their power in the process of change.

In assessing the varying uses of power by therapists (which can be as much to do with their personality as their method) it is necessary to examine what purpose is served. Is it aimed at the empowerment of clients? Is it based on a belief in clients' ability to discover their own path and that they have the capacity to choose their own way of working – what suits them? Most humanistic practitioners have these aims and beliefs, whatever their methodology.

It is not only about putting the client at the centre of the therapeutic process; it is about the inclusion of the therapist as an essential partner in the process. It is not only recognizing the influence that the interventions of the therapist have on the client but also the effect of his personality. It is also being aware of the effect that the client is having on the therapist and using this to assist him to clarify the client's unexpressed needs. Therapists know that the work they do with their clients affects other areas of their own lives. They may experience some negative outcomes. Thus there is a vital need for them to have worked through most of their own issues, have stability in their lives and be able to recognize what their own problems are and which belong to clients. In this, therapists often have to trust their experience and their intuition. In doing this the therapist is seeking to show to the client that he understands. The emphasis is mainly pragmatic. Although there are principles that are implicit in the way therapists work, they are not bound by theories, dogmas or the rigid use of methods.

I would go so far as to say that this is a positive use of counter-transference (the therapist's own issues). The thinking and experience that lie behind this are that most of the harmful effects of childhood that trouble people in later life require a different sort of experience in the present in order to assist clients to deal with their pain. One that liberates them from the belief and attitude that parents have to be right. So the kind of environment in therapy that is capable of countering these early patterns is vital to facilitate growth or change. This new experience is provided by the centrality of the relationship in humanistic psychotherapy.

What are the characteristics of the relationship between a humanistic psychotherapist and his client? It finds and shows a balance between sharing with clients in their needs and being aware that his experience of what is happening between them is separate. This is not easy to define intellectually. It is trusting both self and the other. Being yourself and being with the client. It is a willingness to be close, sometimes confluent and yet knowing the truth that I cannot be you and can only understand you in a limited way. The therapist demonstrates that he will stay with the client without falling over or getting sucked into the client's problems; that he will give of himself in the relationship without pretending that he can solve the client's problems. The word often used to describe the other side of the balance is 'detachment'. This does not quite fit. 'Separateness' is better. As a therapist, I have a separate life in my thoughts, feelings and relationships outside and inside the consulting room.

In his book *Love's Executioner*, Irvin Yalom, an existential psychotherapist who was involved in the setting up of the American Association of Humanistic Psychology, describes the lives of a number of his clients in

such a way that it is clear he was deeply involved with them in their struggles but nevertheless maintained a healthy respect for allowing them to
find their own way.

In the frontispiece of his penetrative analysis of the after-effect of the
'counter culture' Theodore Roszak (1981) describes poetically the nature
of authentic relationships that shows as clearly as anything what the
humanistic therapist is aiming to be.

> You and I . . ..
> we meet as strangers, each carrying a mystery within us.
> I cannot say who you are; I may never know you completely.
> But I trust that you are a person in your own right, possessed of a
> beauty and value that are the Earth's richest treasures.
>
> So I make this promise to you:
> I will impose no identities upon you, but will invite you to become
> yourself without shame or fear.
> I will hold open a space for you in the world and defend your
> right to fill it with an authentic vocation.
> For as long as your search takes, you have my loyalty.

It is not easy to describe the nature of a humanistic therapeutic relationship simply because there are so many disciplines that call themselves
humanistic – at least 15 – and in every one of these each relationship is
central and unique. What I have done is to extrapolate the main features
that might be seen as the central principles to which most within the
humanistic field would subscribe. In the long run, the essence of therapy
is love. What follows is a breakdown of how that is expressed by the
humanistic therapist.

Respect

When a person goes to a therapist, particularly for the first time, she is
likely to feel anxious to a greater or lesser degree. She may put the therapist on an elevated status. She may also be nervous about what she may
reveal of herself. While up to a point this is natural and healthy, the
humanistic therapist does not use this attitude to maintain his own
power. He seeks to put the client at her ease by treating what she says
with respect – whether he, the therapist, likes it or not. That is not to say
the therapist is being phoney, but he avoids expressing his own thoughts
or beliefs so as to leave the client free to be herself. He accepts the client's
freedom and ability to choose how to be and what meaning to live by. Carl
Rogers used the phrase 'unconditional positive regard'.

The humanistic therapist holds the client in great respect. This includes
being non-judgemental, which I think has been misunderstood to mean
that therapist does not have any critical thoughts or his own set of beliefs.
This is patently not true and is quite unrealistic. What Rogers meant was

that the therapist 'prizes' the experience of his client above his own opinions. He also used the phrase 'non-possessive warmth' to indicate that the therapist can have positive feelings towards his clients as long as they don't spill over into controlling. So the therapist learns to monitor his thoughts and feelings so that they do not get in the way. No doubt many humanistic therapists do express their views but hopefully present them as an offer rather than insisting or implying that the client must accept them, and are open for their views not to be accepted. As Voltaire was reputed to have said 'I *may* disapprove of what you say, but I will defend to the death your right to say it' (Tallentyre, 1907). In practice, the humanistic therapist will avoid giving any opinions in the initial stages of the relationship in order to establish the norm that he will always accept the right of the client to have her own thoughts, feelings and beliefs.

There are many injunctions, even training courses, about political correctness in areas of social and work environments, concerning sex, race, class and religion, the essence of which is vital to good relationships. In humanistic work, however, these are implicit in the discipline of giving proper regard to each client as an individual without being rigorous. There are many aspects of clients' lives where this respect is important. For instance their social and religious upbringing and the values they manifest in telling their story may be very different from that of the therapist. More especially, in relating their problems, the way they spend their time and relate to others in their life may not only be difficult to share but on occasions might be repellent to the therapist. The question that can be answered only circumstantially is 'how is it best to respond?' Not to respond may be seen to be uncaring or judgemental. The next characteristic of humanistic psychotherapy will give some clues.

Empathy

The humanistic therapist seeks to allow the experience of another to enter his being. People often want very much to be understood, but understanding is sometimes not possible. To say 'I understand you' is a gesture rather than the truth. As it is essential that the therapist is honest with his clients, he needs to avoid presenting them with a fallacy. Understanding is what I feel when someone listens to me with care. However, what the humanistic therapist offers is empathy based on how he experiences his client and from his own experience. This is not a matter of 'I know how you feel' but 'from what I hear and see from you, and how it resonates with me, I can respond with consideration and feeling'. The tool for doing this is active listening.

Carl Rogers, the father of person-centred therapy, described this neatly in his classic book *On Becoming A Person* (1961) as one of the questions that concerned him about helping relationships. 'Can I let myself enter fully into the world of his feelings and personal meanings and see these as he does?' (p. 53). He talked about the ability to be with another person, to stand in his shoes and to find ways of communicating this, which he admitted was not easy. At times, the therapist will make the right 'noise' or gesture, which will convey this accurately to his client. The phrase 'listening with the third ear' comes to mind. That is, listening to what is going between the words and looking to the feelings that have their own language. The number of times I have asked someone what they are feeling and they reply with 'I am feeling *like* . . .' It is not easy to be accurate about what you are feeling at any given moment. A feeling happens and the therapist seeks to identify with what his client is going through both in the session and in the part of her life that she is recalling. The purpose of empathic listening is to assist the client to find her own meaning. This is a process that takes time. It is not a single response.

Empathy does not, of course, lie solely in the domain of therapy. In fact, it is one of those attitudes that enhances human relationships generally. Most people, however, are rarely cognizant of what it feels like to be someone else. If they were, many of the world's ills, both personal and political, would not happen. The terrorist attack on the USA on 11 September 2001 reminds us of this contradiction, as was so touchingly described by Ian McEwan in the *Guardian* on 14 September 2001:

> we remember what we have seen, and we daydream helplessly. Lately, most of us have inhabited the space between the terrible actuality and these daydreams. Waking before dawn, going about our business during the day, we fantasise ourselves into the events. What if it was me? This is the nature of empathy, to think oneself into the minds of others. These are the mechanics of compassion: you are under the bedclothes, unable to sleep, and you are crouching in the brushed steel lavatory at the rear of the plane, whispering a final message to your loved one. There is only that one thing to say, and you say it. All else is pointless. You have very little time before some holy fool, who believes in his place in eternity, kicks in the door, slaps your head and orders you back to your seat . . . If the hijackers had been able to imagine themselves into the thoughts and feelings of the passengers, they would have been unable to proceed. It is hard to be cruel once you permit yourself to enter the mind of your victim. Imagining what it is like to be someone other than yourself is at the core of our humanity. It is the essence of compassion, and it is the beginning of morality. The hijackers used fanatical certainty, misplaced religious faith, and dehumanising hatred to purge themselves of the human instinct for empathy. Among their crimes was a failure of the imagination. As for their victims in the planes and in the towers, in their terror they would not have felt it at the time, but those snatched and anguished assertions of love were their defiance.

Transparency

The humanistic therapist is willing to be open about what he is experiencing with his clients. What the therapist does, thinks and feels is not to be completely hidden. On the contrary, at times it might be relevant to reveal what the therapist is feeling or thinking. Sidney Jourard (1971) in his book *The Transparent Self* commented that allowing others to see what you are experiencing is a highly effective way of working with people. It is, of course, important that this is not done self-indulgently but rather when it is appropriate. How do you judge appropriateness? Three main criteria are usually helpful:

* when it reflects what the client is talking about;
* when it may be illustrative of the problem she is facing;
* when there are clues from your knowledge of the client's personality that she is likely to make a connection.

There can be no certainty. The response of the client will clearly indicate whether it has been effective. The therapist's skill is to be aware, sometimes very quickly, whether his feelings relate to his own issues or past experiences or whether they are a direct result of what the client is feeling or avoiding.

A person may be saying she has no problems with her workmates and at the same time she is grimacing. The therapist may respond 'I feel tense as you say that', which may elicit from the client 'well to be honest I was thinking of a particular person who never co-operates with me. Every time I see him I get really uptight.' So body language is important. The gestalt therapist places considerable emphasis on this, although he does not interpret it, but invites the client to express what she is experiencing when he notices, for instance, that her foot is moving: 'what is your foot saying?' and the client may respond 'I want to kick my boss!'. Although some humanistic therapists work with the unconscious, the main drift of humanistic psychotherapy is to stay in the present – what is happening in the session between the therapist and the client. What are you doing, remembering, avoiding?

Caring confrontation

Out of his concern, the humanistic therapist confronts what may hinder the client. One of the distinctive behaviours of the humanistic therapist is that he actively supports the client both in her hurt and achievement. In this, he avoids doing things for the client that she can do for herself. When a client is experiencing the pain of loss, the therapist seeks to find a way of holding her in her grief without imagining that he can take her pain away. When a client shares a change in her life, whether this is to do with her problems, some personal growth or success in work or relationships, the therapist cheers her on in a way that fits. It is anathema for the humanistic therapist in such moments to just sit there and do nothing. That is not being humanistic. He takes the risk of the client becoming dependent, but that's all right because if the client didn't become attached to the therapist little of lasting value would be happening. From this basis of regard for the client, however, the other side is that he will not leave unchallenged what is incongruent, without making any judgement. Often confrontation is experienced as judgemental and part of the therapeutic process is the untangling of the client's projections on to the therapist.

There are various methods of confrontation. To be of value they must come from a caring position. Confrontation without care is not only worthless – it is abusive in the sense that it is for the therapist's gratification and not a genuine response to the client's needs. Confrontation is caring where it aims to help the client through his dilemma. It is an offer rather than an imposition. In this aspect of therapy lies one of the core skills of the therapist's work. The way he intervenes into the thinking and feeling constructs by which the client, out of awareness, maintains her difficulty is vital. It is the interaction of the therapist with the client – entering into her struggle to make sense of what she is doing; entering into contention, from a caring position, with how she blocks herself. *How* this is done is vital. It should be done within the framework of a humanistic relationship with respect and empathy.

In his book *Helping the Client*, John Heron (1990) outlines six categories of intervention, one of which he describes as 'confrontation'. In using this word here, all interventions might be regarded as being confrontational. Some are light, some are forceful. The client-centred approach would favour reflection – understanding what the person means and checking it. Following the client and helping her to experience it fully in the present – not just intellectually but emotionally. The gestalt therapist is likely to 'corner' the client by heightening awareness of her power through exaggerating the dilemma. In transactional analysis, the aim would be to focus on contradictions and impasses in order to raise the emotional or mental energy to change. In other, more cathartic-based, therapies confrontation is often very direct and highly challenging of the position the client is adopting. There is not the space to go into more detail about the differing methods of confrontation, but the common aim is to offer a shift in feelings that will highlight and change the person's self-image and attitude to her difficulty.

Experiential

The humanistic therapist validates the experience of his client. How a client experiences her life, both past and present, is integral to the humanistic approach. Although a client may question it, the therapist always supports her in it. Only through her experience will the client be able to learn how to change. Often, just through telling her story, the client discovers some new truth and alleviation of distress. Furthermore whatever the client experiences in the session is validated. The therapist may question his client's interpretation of her experience, only to open up a greater sense of reality for the client.

The focus of humanistic therapy is the client's current life experience rather than past events, which, although they may explain what the client is feeling or thinking either in the immediate present or her current situation, do not of themselves bring resolution. This does not necessarily mean that the therapist ignores the past but that it is not his primary focus.

You might wonder why this is. Partly it is a reaction to analytical therapy but it is also seen that the client is re-experiencing the past when she meets problems in her present life. Often the client becomes increasingly aware of her own picture of herself in the course of the therapeutic process, which is often the central issue. This is most easily recognizable through what she is experiencing either in the relationship with the therapist or in her everyday life when she is having the difficulties for which she has come to receive help.

The ways in which this is addressed may vary from method to method but the essential ingredient is how the client experiences what is bothering her. The humanistic therapist uses his skills to allow and encourage whatever is happening inside the client. For instance, a person may have done something that she feels guilty about. She needs not only to acknowledge this but also to feel the shame in the present and deal with it appropriately. At the same time there also needs to be some addressing of the underlying cause. This may be experienced as a belief, which may be derived from a parent's injunction. This can be dealt with by facilitating the client to re-experience the parental message in the session and making another feeling response that changes her attitude to the cause of her shame. This happens in the session so that the client experiences the change in the present with the help of the therapist. This may take some time if the client is still strongly attached to the parental message and she may need to stay in touch with her present discomfort until she is ready to let go. In gestalt therapy this is called 'dialoguing' and can be a powerful way of experiencing blocks in the past and present impasses that keep the client stuck in her feelings and behaviours that are either no longer relevant, or are preventing the client taking action in the present to resolve her issues.

Autonomy

The humanistic therapist invites the client to take responsibility for herself. This is meant to be not directive but realistic. We are, as individuals, responsible for ourselves – for what we think, feel and do. We are not, and do not need to be, victims. We share a part in whatever difficulties we encounter – even tragedy. To begin with, a client may find this hard. Part of her dilemma may be expressed as 'why is this happening to me?' In the long run the therapist is saying 'you are in charge of your life'. Likewise, the therapist takes responsibility for what he does.

This is seen to be a fundamental premiss. Although we may try to avoid owning responsibility for our lives, in the long run we cannot pass this on to others, God or the universe. Blaming others is a common way that people avoid the discomfort of their own existence. In this respect, we are all alone inside our skin. No one really knows what is going on inside us. Furthermore, no one else can change it, even under extreme mental torture. Often people turn to drugs to change the way they feel, but they cannot escape themselves. In fact, quite the opposite. These exaggerate the dilemma, which can be relieved only by another fix.

When people come into therapy they are often (without knowing it) angry with someone who has let them down in the past – someone whom they believe had some sort of responsibility for their well-being. There is a lot of blame or shame and it takes time for the therapist to build up enough trust to confront this and the pain of the client's dilemma. Although this is clear when the person is dead, there may be a lot of unexpressed anger that needs to be discharged before the client can see and feel that it is her life now and that she can deal with the loss, taking responsibility for what she did or didn't do or, alternatively, that she can blame the other for what she is left with. Any distraction on to another only prolongs the discomfort. This, of course, is not limited to those who have died. Often it is even harder to release oneself from people and events that are still around. While the humanistic therapist empathizes with the hurt, he does not collude with the client in either feeling sorry for herself or letting her play 'if it weren't for you'. The invitation is to feel the pain and the anger of what has happened, accept the effects and let go of the resentment, guilt and negative beliefs.

The central teaching of contribution training (1998), developed by Peter Fleming, is that we make a conscious and unconscious contribution to everything in the way we use our energy. Although we do not have the power to change much of what happens outside us, each of us makes a contribution by what we do. By becoming aware of this, we can change how we think, feel and act. One of the aims of humanistic psychotherapy is to help the client to realize her own sense of autonomy. Ultimately, it is probably not possible to achieve complete autonomy. There are things that affect us that we cannot avoid. Our freedom is limited by external events. Our ability to find fulfilment is hindered by the past – our upbringing and our decisions. But in the present we can accept responsibility for what we do with these phenomena – whatever that is. This is not just an idealistic notion: the greater the sense of autonomy, the better chance we have to find peace with ourselves and the world.

To move from being dependent on the environment – whether it be on people or on material things – to being dependent on oneself is self-reliance or self-support. It is not self-sufficiency, which is not needing anyone. There is a healthy and realistic level of dependence that needs to be encouraged in clients, especially those who have a problem with trust. At the same time, it can be misplaced and then they have to find another path. In this way they can discover how to use the environment for their nurture and maintenance without making themselves ultimately reliant on it: they can have their expectations and let go of them. They can learn to ask and give to others, or not. They can learn how to deal with what is given and how to deal with disappointments without losing themselves in others.

Centred on personal growth

The humanistic therapist assists clients to grow in their own way. The model of humanistic psychology is that the process of therapy is about growth. Although people may come into therapy to deal with a problem or their bad feelings, the outcome is often different from what they expect. It sets them off on a journey of self-exploration that can lead to greater self-awareness and self-acceptance. Hopefully, as a result of therapy, clients will be more effective in managing themselves and their interactions with others. It is more important that they will realize that they have the resources to achieve their potential relevant to their needs. They can discover hidden parts of themselves that may be either shocking or expansive. The humanistic therapist may at times push the client beyond her level of comfort in order to break through a barrier of pain that can release her from her limitations.

In therapy, this development is implicit in clients opening up to more possibilities for themselves. Humanistic psychology has always included spirituality in its theory. This is described by some as transpersonal – what is outside the realms of empirical evidence – the hopes and dreams that enable people to aspire to that which at the moment may be beyond them. I like the term 'higher self' used in psychosynthesis because it holds on to what is observable while using it to help people discover things outside of reason and perception. In this model, people can experience abundance in their lives that is not necessarily limited by their material circumstances.

Maslow expounded the idea of the 'self-actualizing person', who, at the highest level of his human needs had what he called 'peak' experiences. In one sense, these are more likely to occur when the 'lower' needs have been met, but there is a contradiction there. People are able to appreciate beauty, truth and love in any state of physical well-being. Ecstasy, as John Rowan (2001) noted, can be felt in response to ordinary things. Prosperity and freedom are not restricted to the wealthy, the better educated, more sophisticated or the politically powerful. It can be quite common in primitive tribes to visit the places of knowing and richness. In reality, the concept of the fully functioning person is a bit of a myth. Although we may support our clients in reaching out for more in their lives, we also need to guard against the holy grail syndrome and learn to experience what is 'enough'.

This, then, is the backdrop of humanistic therapy and in moments of enlightenment the whole perspective of a person can change, often out of something apparently quite trivial. It is therefore not the cleverness or knowledge of the therapist that is the key to growth. It is the openness, which the therapeutic relationship, based on humanistic principles and beliefs, offers for change.

Self-awareness

The humanistic therapist encourages clients to be aware of themselves. Being aware of self is the key to anything that a client may want to change in herself. This is different from the experience of self-consciousness, which is usually inhibiting and arises from self-criticism. In being self-aware, there is no judgement. Through and in it, is the essence of learning. The therapist simply offers a way for the client to pay attention to how she is being herself.

Fritz Perls, the originator of gestalt therapy, insisted that people stay in the 'here and now' as this, he pointed out, is the only reality. Apart from staying in the immediate present, there are three main possible activities in the here and now – remembering, anticipating or fantasizing – all of which involve imagining something that is not happening except inside the person. That is the reality that the humanistic approach seeks to encourage; what is going on now inside a person, not what is going on here outside a person now. One of the fruitful exercises that came out of encounter groups is to invite people to look around themselves or to physically feel a person or an object and then to be aware of what they are experiencing as they do this. This stimulates a sense of self and the environment.

The therapist not only invites self-awareness in his clients but also, just as importantly, with himself. It is the way in which the therapist uses his sense of self that is the key to the humanistic approach. The client is not an object and the therapist is not a mechanic. If the aim of the therapy is to help people to be themselves as fully as possible, then that also applies to the way in which the therapist views himself. As we have already noted, the key element in humanistic therapy is the way in which the therapist uses himself in the process. This makes certain demands on him to be true to himself and to share that awareness directly or indirectly with his clients. In turn, this is likely to be a model for the client. Therefore, many of the interventions will be directed to assisting self-awareness. For example: 'What are you feeling now?' 'You appear to be troubled.' 'I am experiencing some discomfort about what you have just said, are you?' 'How did you get into this place?' 'What are you aware of now you realize the effect of your actions?' 'How are you stopping yourself?' 'See if you can find a way to change that.' 'Check what you are experiencing in your body.' 'What are you avoiding?' These kinds of intervention are aimed at helping clients to discover resources of energy they are not aware of, whether positive or negative. How they can use them emerges from the new sense of themselves.

These are the core principles of the therapeutic relationship in humanistic practice. They are the foundations for establishing and maintaining a close person-to-person working relationship. It is grounded unashamedly in affection, without which it becomes merely a procedure. No doubt there are other features that some would include in their particular method of working. In Part Four, a group of humanistic therapists describe their particular ways of working, which will give the reader some idea of the breadth, nature and quality of the humanistic approach.

Chapter 7
The humanistic therapist as a person

Humanistic therapy depends on three interrelated factors: the skills of the therapist, the trust of the client, and the personal characteristics of the therapist. It is the recognition of this last factor that makes the difference in humanistic therapy. The way in which the therapist's behaviour reveals his attitudes about himself, his life and people is what the client experiences most powerfully in their meeting. Here is a list of attributes most of which a humanistic therapist possesses:

- He has a passion about the human condition and a genuine interest in human growth – both that of others and his own.
- He has a commitment to his own development as a person. Being humanistic is not merely his professional practice. It is a way of life for him. He is continually paying attention to his own quality of life and using his wide range of resources to enhance his own growth through self-awareness.
- He has dealt with the major issues in his life. This does not mean that he doesn't have problems – everyone, however mature and developed, has problems. What it does mean is that he has undertaken extensive personal therapy in individual and group work and worked through his own personality patterns. This experience of his own personal growth has taken him into his own inner world to discover and resolve the particular difficulties he has both inside himself and in the way he relates to others. In brief, he will know what kind of a person he is. He recognizes his unfinished business and his potential blind spots. In the course of this he actively discovers things about himself that other people would hardly need to know. As I used to say to my students: 'make sure your clients are not the first to find out important things about you before you do.'
- He is aware of his own limitations. This involves working within his own competence and training. There are types of client problems that he may not be able to help, either through lack of experience or simply because he knows that he is just not cut out emotionally in some areas. For instance, in my own practice, I am wary of people with addic-

tive behaviour and I will not work with children. However, I know I am good with those who experience depressive or compulsive feelings. I am able to offer support and options for change in work and personal relationships.

- He recognizes that he has his own agenda, both emotional and motivationally. He knows what he wants for his clients and is watchful to avoid making this his aim rather than what *they* want. He is clear about what drives him in his work – his ulterior motives – so that he does not impose them on his clients in his care for them.

- He is aware of the risks involved in being a therapist. There are occupational hazards and hardships, emotionally, physically and mentally, as well as those that are often imposed on his family. Often we are more humane with our clients than with our loved ones.

- He has developed ways to protect himself from the negative effects of the work, through his friends, his supervisor and colleagues, as well as constantly reviewing his practice using the resources of his professional association. He listens to himself and talks to himself. He uses his own techniques to help him keep a balance to the distortions to which his work subjects him.

- He invites and takes in feedback from his clients. It is important for him to 'hear' what they are saying to him whether he invites it or not.

- He has stability in his personal life. Of course this is not an all-time guarantee because crises can hit the most self-actualized person. In this case he will know, through his support network and self-awareness, whether it is time to stop practising and take a break.

- He has interests and activities outside his work in which he is treated like an ordinary person. This may take various forms. One of the problems of being a therapist is that the intensity of his work with people in sessions is both so demanding and so absorbing that relationships in other settings can seem banal. Often a therapist works unsociable hours and it requires discipline to ensure that he has proper breaks and holidays.

- He has experience in a range of human activities other than therapy. Ideally this is a second profession. Many therapists have been involved in other human relations jobs before training. The variety of occupations that colleagues of mine have been in before becoming therapists is quite amazing, ranging from priests to furniture removers.

- He likes himself and enjoys the way he lives his life and his work with people.

- He has experience of other forms of therapy other than the primary method in which he has been trained. There are a number of training agencies that actively encourage their trainees to participate in other methods. Unfortunately there are some that discourage it. One of the strengths of the Association of Humanistic Psychology Practitioners is that it is willing to accredit therapists who have a number of different trainings.

- It is important that he gives recognition to other approaches and methods, recognizing that his own way of working and choice of method are those that he thinks are the best for him, rather than those that he considers to be 'the right way'. Experienced practitioners in any discipline will realize that different people are happy with different approaches – both clients and therapists
- He is watchful of becoming emotionally dependent on his clients. To say he is not dependent on them is a delusion. He depends on them for his income, his professional satisfaction and for a degree of emotional fulfilment. In this mutual dependency he has a lot to offer his clients, and he also gains a lot, not the least in learning about the myriad forms of being human. As the nature of his work is highly personal, he is bound to form some degree of attachment to those he works with and therefore gains nourishment from the encounter. It is important to stress that although the reasons that most therapists are engaged in such a demanding practice are selfish, this only helps to underline the equality that is essentially humanistic. Of course we put our clients' needs first in the way we treat them, but not exclusively. Both are essential and intertwined and are connected directly to the personal lifestyle and attitude of the therapist. My teacher once said to me that a measure of his success was that his work and life were coming closer together.

The work of being a therapist does not require any particular personality profile, but anyone who lasts in this business will have considerable emotional strength, commitment, a positive attitude to life and will trust his intuition.

One of the features of humanistic training is that of personal development. Every trainee is bound to enter therapy and continue his own growth, working through his own issues. Often a person contemplating becoming a psychotherapist in the humanistic field will already be in counselling or therapy. Many are already interested in personal development and have benefited from the experience. This can be ongoing through life or undertaken periodically.

Chapter 8
The other side

The previous chapter may have painted an idealistic picture of the humanistic therapist, but things happen in the work and life of even the most well-developed practitioner that can distort his perception. Nearly all psychotherapists are working because they are committed to helping people and, for the most part, are well motivated in their relationships with their clients. They are rigorous and conscientious in their practice, and attempt to maintain an open and hassle-free service to their clients. Most of them feel a sense of dedication or vocation in their chosen career, which for many has been tested in another helping profession prior to therapy – teaching, nursing, social and community work, the Church, and so forth. Parallel with these positive intentions, and working within the principles set out above, there is always going to be *the other side.* By that I mean the aspects of the therapist's personality that have alternative motives, hidden agendas or plain misguided or unskilful behaviour. For the most part he has worked through these in his training and continues to focus on them with his supervisor.

In the introduction to his manual for counsellors, Gerard Egan (1994) talks about the 'shadow side' of helping and then goes on to include a section in each chapter on managing this at each stage in the therapeutic process. He defines the 'shadow side' as: 'All those things that adversely affect the helping relationship and process, its outcomes, and its impact in substantive ways but that are not identified and explored by helper or client.' He cites impure motives, incompetence, games, hidden agendas, unbeneficial methods, decision-making and going nowhere, as these are out of the awareness of both client and therapist. Egan pays a lot of attention to the primary causes and manifestations of the shadow side. It could be said that the effectiveness of humanistic therapy is that it stresses self-development. One of the chief causes of unsatisfactory therapeutic relationships lies in the self-importance of the therapist's role and the rigidity that can set into the process. This can happen to the inexperienced therapist through keeping strictly to the 'rules' he has been taught and his own lack of self-confidence, or it can creep into the experienced practitioner's work through overfamiliarity with his way of working. This can result in lack of spontaneity, being phoney and patronizing. He points out that clients share the shadow side. They are not as vulnerable as they seem. Just reading Egan's descriptions of the 'shadow side' is a useful deterrent.

Similarly, John Heron (1990) has a whole chapter on what he calls called 'degenerate and perverted' interventions and ways of overcoming them. This is worthwhile reading for self-study. He lists four kinds of degenerate interventions: unsolicited, manipulative, compulsive and unskilled. Like Egan, he is not ascribing these to deliberate behaviours from the helper in most cases, but rather views them as due to a lack of training or awareness. He goes on to list, with uncanny precision, a telling number of ways in which therapists can be unhelpful. The problem with this approach to dealing with the negative aspects of therapy is that it can stem from and lead to an attitude of self-distrust. We know about the concepts of dark and light, good and evil, right and wrong, ying and yang and so the words shadow, degenerate, and dark, while useful metaphors, are meaningless except in the context of a given approach and relationship. I know when I have cut a piece of wood whether it is straight. That, however, is only relevant to any given application.

So in this section I choose to avoid using these words because I think they are part of the problem, not because I don't know that hurt and possibly harm can result in therapy. Humanistic psychotherapy is humanistic because it allows for error and recognizes that 'getting it right' may not necessarily be helpful. In saying this, I want to distinguish between error and actions that are deliberately harmful or careless about the rights of the client arising from the perverted self-interest of the therapist. Although there are ethical codes and complaints procedures for dealing with these, they can only be a deterrent. All humanistic practitioners have to be aware of the risks and monitor their behaviour rigorously; listen to themselves, their clients, their supervisors, colleagues and friends and have the humility and proper sense of self that trusts the process going on between client and therapist.

One of the features of humanistic practice is that of continuing professional development. Although this will include ongoing training and supervision, this dimension of the therapist's work is often very subtle and it requires constant attention. All therapists need to know in what ways they are likely to be less than helpful but there are occasions when what might be considered in the cold light of day as a hindrance can prove to be the opposite. Now a lot of this could be consigned to the concept of counter-transference – to which are attributed those aspects, feelings, thoughts or actions towards the client that are a result of the therapist's unresolved early experiences. Carl Rogers more or less rejected transference as a working model because it tends to leave the therapist as an object rather than a person.

Petrŭska Clarkson (1995, p.160) mentions three types of personal agenda:

- The therapist's feelings and emotional responses: proactive counter-transference is an intrusion of the therapist's own past or significant others into the psychotherapeutic relationship.
- Reactive counter-transference is the ghostly evocation of the client's past experiences or significant others into the consulting room.
- That which is left is the person-to-person; two authentic, integrated adults who have autonomous, separate, independent, here-and-now feelings and emotions.

This is based on the analytical model of transference, which humanistic therapists either take or leave. It is not a phenomenon but a concept.

Both client and therapist are part of the same process. They are both walking around in the dark. Although the humanistic therapist is used to this experience, it is no use pretending that he doesn't have his fears. We must stop deluding ourselves that therapy is one OK person relating to another not-OK person. Using the best of ourselves and the worst of ourselves, we enter into an unknown country. This is a useful analogy. My country is foreign to them. Their country is foreign to me. If I am talking to someone from another country, it is not from a position of being totally knowledgeable about my own country – only my experience of it. I can find out about them by listening empathetically. They find out about me by the way I treat them.

There are bound to be aspects of any therapist's work and any professional's work that are influenced by their experience, both good and bad, by their beliefs and current life situations. This can be an obstacle if it is out of awareness, and a positive contribution if it is in awareness. Sometimes accidental 'mistakes' are experienced by clients as a learning. I remember one occasion in a group when I was very tired and finding it hard to concentrate. I found myself going off and hearing only parts of what was being said. To my surprise my client said she felt much clearer about her depressed state and the elation was obvious. She said that was the best piece of work she had done with me. The outcomes of therapy are not all down to the therapist. Sometimes clients get better in spite of the therapist! That is why in humanistic psychotherapy the direction is always in favour of the client. The therapist can invite and encourage his clients to value and take responsibility for themselves, to have their feelings, to be open and be aware of self, but these can never be 'musts'. If a client is unwilling to do these things then that's up to her and it is unlikely that she will want to stay in humanistic therapy.

This leads on to another aspect of the 'other side' of therapy – that of when to end and how this is decided. Ideally, this is a joint decision between therapist and client. It is vital but not always easy for a therapist to support clients when they want to leave. He may have 'good' reasons in his view of clients' problems and needs for holding on to them but he must always let them go. By all means, he can give his opinion but not in order to pressure them to stay. This process can become tangled up with the livelihood of the therapist. True, the therapist has to take into account his own needs to support himself financially, but provided that he has made clear the terms of leaving, money issues should not come into the equation.

Going on from this is another part of the 'other side'. How much does he charge? How much does he expect to earn? Although he is dependent on clients for his living, he is, at the same time, providing a valuable service (admittedly to those who can afford it). At the same time, issues about money are rarely talked about in professional circles. This is a subject for debate and raises profound issues about how a therapist values himself and his work.

Again, why do so many humanistic therapists follow the analytical habit of 50-minute hours? What an absurd doublethink! Is the idea to get more clients into a day's work? What is the maximum number of clients per day, per week, for effective work to avoid burnout? The answer to these questions will vary according to each therapist's situation or temperament. But they raise issues about what is the basis for doing therapy. To feel important? To pay the mortgage? Because it is an enjoyable and fulfilling occupation? When I was a tutor in counselling one of the questions at the end of the first year was 'leaving aside altruism, what are your ordinary human reasons for choosing to be a counsellor?' The range of answers was astonishing. Some found that the difficulty of doing the work was far too much to justify their ulterior motives.

I am aware that, in this section, I have moved through a number of issues briefly – each of which could easily form a separate chapter. There is not the space to cover these in any detail – only to indicate how the human side of doing psychotherapy is vitally important within the total endeavour of offering professional help to people in the emotional difficulties of their lives.

In Jeffrey Kottler's (1990) book, *On Being a Therapist*, he wonders if any therapist really considered the risks of doing the personally demanding work of a humanistic therapist he would do it at any price. Being a therapist requires a certain sort of sane madness. Carl Whitaker (1989), in his reflections on his life and work as a family therapist, comments: 'The isolation required of the therapeutic setting allows for a kind of craziness without the isolation that makes ordinary crazy experiences so frightening. It is craziness with a valid boundary supplied by the professional other' (p.151). Without this facility, it is doubtful whether the extraordinary nature of psychotherapy would be viable. The humanistic therapist needs to be in touch with his 'other side'. With careful monitoring, it can be beneficial to clients; without it, the therapy can involve 'wild goose chases'.

Masson (1990) contends that the precondition of therapy is the therapists' view of their clients' problems in terms of their own theories. The cause of corruption lies in their own ideas of health. Although most of the targets of his attack on psychotherapy are in the field of psychoanalysis, he turns to humanistic therapy with a chapter on Carl Rogers, citing his paternalism and criticizing Rogers' core conditions as myths. He draws attention to the fact that, no matter how humane therapy is, it is still open to abuse because he believes that any therapy distorts people's reality. It is important that any psychotherapist is open to question anything he has been taught and to encourage his clients to do the same. One of my teachers, Eoin O'Leary, constantly said to his clients: 'Don't believe anything I say. Believe yourself.'

Therapists and clients are all in the same pot. We share a common humanity. We are not angels. In the last resort, humanistic therapy is an attitude to people and to self that takes into account the other side of being human.

So humanistic therapy depends upon a positive view of people, the creative nature of the way in which the therapist relates to his clients, and the kind of person he is. In the film *Bicentennial Man*, Alex the robot, who wants to become a human, is told by his lover 'Human beings are a mess. The trouble with you is that you are perfect.' It is this recognition that spurs the humanistic therapist. A Methodist minister's son in the nineteenth century went to Glasgow bent on converting the people in the Gorbals. After a year he wrote to his father saying 'I came here to change them. Instead they have changed me. I no longer want to change them. I like them the way they are.' It is this truth that motivates the humanistic therapist. Of course, he wants to help people but only if they want to be helped and only in the way they discover they want his help. The change happens because something happens in the process of their meeting based on feeling heard, accepted and loved.

PART THREE
KEY ISSUES FOR HUMANISTIC PSYCHOTHERAPY

Chapter 9
Contradictions

It is in the nature of humanistic psychotherapy that it is open to the contradictory nature of experience. It accepts polarities – both sides of the story, both ends of the spectrum. This part is devoted to examining some of the issues that challenge the humanistic approach and how it seeks to find the truth that lies somewhere in the midst of contradictions. The essential aspect of the humanistic therapist's work is to explore what is here, what is present, what is, how you are, and how I am, as the journey of life and existence rolls out before us.

Its taken me this long to see the truth unravel,
It was here down in the hedgerows of the winding path I travel.
(Phillip Goodhand-Tait)

So humanistic psychotherapy is always alternative, looking at all the possibilities, being creative in response to people's pain – so that it reflects the uncertainty of life. It avoids dogmatic adherence to method and programmes for change. It questions appearances, at the same time seeing the truth in superficialities as manifestations of what is happening.

It recognizes that what seems to be the goal often has a subtext that produces unexpected outcomes.

And there's no need for turning back
For all roads lead to where I stand
And I believe we'll walk them all
No matter what we may have planned.
(Don McClean)

There are no straight lines in life or in the process of therapy. Everyone's path is different. The therapist is prepared to be surprised not only by his clients but by his own response. As Yalom (1989) realized when faced with the person, his preconceptions went out of the window. 'I do not like to work with patients who are in love . . . yet Thelma in the opening minutes of our first interview, told me that she was hopelessly, tragically in love, and I never hesitated not for one moment, to accept her into treatment' (p. 15). He believed he could help her out of her pain.

John Rowan (2001) sees the core of humanistic psychology in paradox and the nature of its thinking as dialectical – that is, change is of the essence of life and that the process of change lies in the connection between opposites such as love and hate, darkness and light. The outcome of this approach is that nothing is fixed or final and this determines the need for spontaneity and holds things in a healthy tension.

So in this part of the book, I shall explore how these contradictions apply to some issues in therapy – theory and experience, truth and facts, logic and paradox, thought and feelings. In the centre of this is the essence of human existence – the positive struggle to make personal sense of both the joy and the pain of life. The purpose is to help people to find their own understanding, meaning and the best way to be themselves.

I have chosen six issues – three concerning the *structure* of the work – in the role of therapist, in training, and in accreditation; and three about the *quality* of the work – the spiritual dimension, the nature of contact in therapy, and the underlying motivation for being humanistic – love. This part demonstrates that humanistic therapy is personal, its training is a whole experience, its competence is a self-monitoring integrity, it leaves space for something that cannot be explained, it maintains emotional contact, it values people's feelings and it is grounded in love.

Chapter 10
Being oneself in the role of psychotherapist

In a thought-provoking book, Petrūska Clarkson (1995) identifies five possible modalities of the therapeutic relationship:

- the working alliance;
- the transferential/countertransferential relationship;
- the reparative/developmentally-needed relationship;
- the person-to-person relationship;
- the transpersonal relationship.

The primary mode in humanistic practice is the person-to-person relationship based on a working alliance taking into account transpersonal experiences, although some humanistic therapists would include other modes. While Clarkson's framework of the multidimensional nature of psychotherapy is highly illuminating and inclusive, it tends to blur the distinctive difference in perception of what is happening in the various disciplines. As I put it to an analyst friend of mine, 'what you and I are doing is something different'.

The humanistic approach has regarded the use of transference as the antithesis of the real relationship that occurs between the therapist and the client. Transference is the projection of infantile wishes and fears on the therapeutic relationship as a way for the client to gain insight and resolution. The concepts of projection and introjection in gestalt therapy seem to be capable of being dealt with more realistically *in* the relationship. Projection is experiencing my own feeling or potential for action as being the property of someone else. Introjection is the passive assimilation of others' feelings or beliefs as belonging to me. These are avoidances from what is actually happening in the present and can be confronted within the therapeutic relationship and owned.

Carl Rogers repudiated the transferential model because it puts the attitudes to parental experiences, which we all have, into a therapeutic context and puts the therapist into a position of authority and gives him power which he does not have or, if he does, it is prone to misuse. Fritz Perls confronted clients who put him in a superior place as being 'phoney'. The client has power and it is the job of the therapist to make her aware of it. Otherwise, as Eric Berne pointed out, games like 'you're wonderful, professor' can easily be played. In most humanistic practice clients are invited to share their feelings and thoughts about the therapist. The humanistic therapist sees his task to help people out of their feelings of helplessness and unworthiness; to resolve these feelings in the here-and-now relationship or through dialogue with the client's internalized parents. Although it is likely that the therapist has more knowledge and skill in personal matters, it does not follow that this makes him better. On the contrary, many of us learn much from our clients and, if we are open to them, then we will admit our limitations. The profession of psychotherapy needs to be really honest with itself about what it is capable of delivering. All this is said to question the transferential model, as it is based on fantasy. Those who use this model recognize this, but nevertheless use it as the basis for their work. Now I know that a number of therapists who would regard themselves as humanistic accept this model, but it is worth considering whether or not this supports a humanistic approach. However, it is not the purpose of this book to criticize the way in which practitioners work – only to support the central beliefs and conditions that have been established and developed by the growth movement.

The major point about the way in which the humanistic therapist acts is that *he is being himself.* Although he is aware that he may remind his client of other relationships, he seeks to discourage any role that is not authentic. The meeting with his client is reality based and the focus is primarily on the present. He is not the role. 'I am playing me in this role.'

One of the values of humanistic group work is that it reduces the focus on the therapist. He is clearly the leader, but there are potentially therapeutic contributions from other members of the group. As the nature of these kind of groups is interactive, the therapist is seen more clearly as a person in a social context. Provided the leader is facilitative and not dominant, the group setting avoids some of the artificial intensity of individual therapy. As one person said of my groups, 'they are like real life'. Perls once said the purpose of therapy is to waken people up out of their dreams and fantasies, which keep them stuck in their neuroses – their pictures of the world through their negative feelings. A teacher of mine, Graham Barnes, said in a lecture at a European conference that taking therapy out of the closeted one-to-one relationship into an open group was the most radical move in therapy since it began.

There is a contradiction in humanistic psychology between the essential ordinariness of both life and the process of therapy – and the way in which people are and can be is extraordinary. There are moments of ecstasy and enlightenment but these are not going to happen every session. We need to be constantly on guard against the unreal expectations of clients, which, in the long run, are unhelpful. So the style of humanistic therapy is personalistic. The role is one of being there for another – face to face. One of the important departures from psycho-analysis was that the therapist was fully present – visible to the client (not out of sight). The therapist shows himself. The client can see what he is doing, the expressions on his face, his posture. The client feels that the therapist is included in the process of the work.

In the consulting room there is no place for superimposing theory, or pretending that you can do anything more than be the best that you can be as a person, using your experience, feelings and thoughts with skill. Many in the field regard therapy as more of an art than as science. That I know the characteristics of schizophrenia and how it is treated doesn't necessarily help me to engage with my client. Knowledge is useful but it is secondary to the human considerations of the person I am and how I treat the people who come for my help.

In humanistic therapy a lot depends on the personality of the therapist in being able to be open to experiencing whatever his clients bring, allow-ing it to affect him; getting involved in their struggle and pain but not overwhelmed by it, although that can happen sometimes. He notices his feelings about his client and uses them (not rejecting them) as part of the process. What the therapist feels in the present moment and as he recalls his own experiences (labelled counter-transference) is all part of the process in the humanistic approach from which change can happen. In discussing the place of feelings in therapy in my book *What is Transactional Analysis?* (1993, p. 48) I sought to differentiate how they could be regarded and used:

> When I am working with clients, I am constantly checking out how I feel. Is it something to do with me?
>
> Is it a genuine response to what the client is doing?
>
> Does it belong to me? or am I experiencing some feeling which the client is avoiding?
>
> I do not hesitate to express my feelings if they fit what is happening – quite often I discover that what I am experiencing is the client's forbidden feel-ing in response to his racket. Sufficient to say here, that the therapeutic relationship provides permission for people to experience their real feel-ings and to express what they feel in a safe environment.

We may well ask to what extent is this a *real* relationship if one person is constantly checking his own behaviour. It is different and it is special because one person is there for the other in way that rarely happens else-where. How much is it a two-way process? How much does the therapist reveal about himself? We shall address these questions in a later section on contact and boundaries.

Chapter 11
Training and development

Being an effective humanistic psychotherapist is one of the most person-ally demanding professions. It requires having a character that can be flexible, spontaneous and open, and being exposed to a certain kind of training. It is here that the natural abilities of a person are deeply influ-enced. Training can give the opportunities for these to flourish. It also requires a background in the helping professions or some equivalent life experience. It is important that prospective therapists have 'bumped around in life a bit' before entering the rarefied atmosphere of training and practice. Ideally psychotherapy is a second career. At the same time applicants for training should not necessarily be barred purely on the basis of lack of academic qualifications. One of the enrichments, in my experience, of training counsellors was the diversity of experience that people brought to the course – a veritable *Yellow Pages* of occupations.

There are many reasons for people deciding to embark on training to be a therapist such as: dissatisfaction with their job and thinking that being a therapist is a preferable career; what used to be called a sense of vocation; an experience of life where this seems to be a natural next step; a way to resolve personal problems. No doubt everyone has mixed motives. One of the purposes of training is to be aware of these and use them as a part of personal development.

Is a good therapist born or made? Like all occupations, it is a bit of both. Without the 'characteristics' described in Part Two, training will only be of limited value. But raw ability needs intense training that will refine, strengthen and extend any natural gifts. Those who are highly motivated and have the gift will become competent regardless of the training, but the training is vital to ensure that good physical health habits, emotional self-discipline and personal growth, trust in oneself and belief in the essential worth of people (including oneself) are encouraged. The skills of combining observation, strategy, intervention and containment are hard to develop. The questions that a trainee (and any therapist) needs to constantly ask himself are:

• Who am I?

- Who are you?
- What do I need to know?
- Why am I here?
- What am I doing here?
- What are you doing here?

The answers to these questions will not be found from anyone else or in books, although there may be clues from other people's experience. So the primary need for training is that of developing the ability to give attention, maintain contact and respond congruently. There are plenty of techniques and concepts that will help but the source of these skills lies within the trainee, and his learning will most likely be enhanced through heightened experience in the training group.

The training of psychotherapists is unlike that of most other professions. Although there is a considerable amount of academic work, there is, in humanistic training, a great emphasis laid on exposure to experiential group work, practice, live supervision and personal development. There is a sense that trainees are being trained to perform, and in that respect becoming a humanistic psychotherapist is more like being trained as an actor, musician or dancer. As Brecht said:

> You (actor) must master the art of observation, before all other arts. For what matters most is not how you look but what you have seen and can show us. What is worth knowing is what you know – the art of observation applied to man is but a branch of dealing with men. Your task is to be explorers and teachers of the art of dealing with people knowing their nature and demonstrating it. You teach them to deal with themselves. You teach the great art of living together.

This is the heart of the matter. It is more 'being' than 'doing' that affects the therapeutic outcome. The skills required by artists can be only partly taught. In truth, the prospective humanistic psychotherapist trains himself. He is responsible for his own learning and development in the same way that the therapist seeks to assist his clients in theirs. This must include using the humanistic approach in the training process. He will learn more about humanistic psychotherapy in the *way* the training is managed than by what information he learns. When I was a tutor in counselling, I constantly kept in mind what effect my style of training was likely to have on the way that the trainee counsellors would practise with their clients. How much I was helping them to internalize humanistic principles by the way I treated them. For instance, I didn't like marking them because that implied judgement. I was happy to comment on their work and to invite them to assess themselves.

Academic requirements should not impede this principle of self-direction. Gerald Egan, one of the exponents of humanistic counselling, questioned whether academic institutions were the appropriate environment for the training of counsellors and therapists – simply because they have tangential objectives. For example, how can grades be given for skills practice? Academic assessment does not fit the vital dynamic of the group and peer assessment. Another problem with academic courses is that they can inhibit the trainee from taking whatever time he needs to complete.

All this is based on the humanistic principle of leaving people free to choose. The trainee is in charge of his own training, just as the client is in charge of her own therapy. I cannot emphasize too strongly that the closer the nature of the training resembles the practice of humanistic psychotherapy, the better.

> The emphasis on the individuality of the trainee is reflected in the emphasis on the individuality of the client. In a sense, to be congruent with the integrative idea that every client is uniquely different, the training needs to model how every trainee is encouraged to grow and develop in a unique and particular way. *In a sense there can be no one training in integrative therapy since the training of psychotherapists at this level of sophistication is necessarily different for each trainee.* Where appropriate, exceptions to regulations or structures are made in creative ways in order to encourage the participation and development of exceptional individuals. The very values of integrative psychotherapy mitigate against mass-produced training and this emphasis stresses that the integration of self precedes any training in integrative theory. The self of the therapist becomes the integrating instrument and the core self the primary integrative factor so that strategies and techniques and theoretical ideas are not haphazardly acquired 'tools' but become 'blood and gesture'. (Clarkson, 1995, p. 283)

Again, you do not learn how to be a therapist by being told how to do it, or by reading books, but through experience. One model expounded by Richard Mowbray (1995) – that of the 'apprentice' working alongside a more experienced 'craftsperson' – seems to be more appropriate than the programmes where a theoretical set of principles are taught, learned and then applied. I am not saying that learning from others, be they teachers or writers great and small, is not important, but it is not primary. Status needs and economic considerations have crept into the training process, often dictating the style. That is fine, provided that the same rigour of humanistic principles is applied. So, in summary, humanistic training is person centred by its nature.

This takes us back to the nature of training. Here are some principles that I have learned from being a group-work trainer, through my own extensive training, through teaching counselling and supervision for over 20 years.

The first factor lies in the trainers themselves. One assumes that all have been practitioners of the method they are teaching. In addition to this, they need to have a high level of communication skills as well as being stable in their own work, able to be flexible, take criticism and handle group dynamics. Another factor is where authority lies. Is it external? In this case, the sponsoring body needs to be in sympathy with the humanistic objectives of the course, including allowing the trainers to use their own discretion about the training within the agreed prospectus. Alongside this, the trainees need to be included in the process of decision-making.

The central teaching method most closely related to humanistic practice is group work, and this forms the bedrock of most therapy training courses. The reason for this is twofold. One is that it provides a democratic arena. Second, it gives the trainees an extended experience of interpersonal activity where their peers can challenge a lot of their assumptions:

> The relationship between individuals in the training group becomes another matrix for intellectual, experiential and emotional learning and experimentation concerning the management of different contrasting, complementary or overarching frames of reference. The polarities of conviction versus uncertainty both serve to deepen understanding of the field and challenge presuppositions as long as neither become fixed or fickle . . . It is considered as important to have and defend strong convictions as it is essential to be willing to question and perhaps even relinquish them. (Clarkson, 1995, p. 283)

An open group format is one the best ways of developing self-awareness. During the course of training it would be a great advantage to have an extended encounter group led by an outside expert in this field. It cannot be emphasized enough that group work is not only a challenging method of learning but also may well be included as a professional skill essential to humanistic work.

So far, I have not mentioned anything about the *content* of training because it is the structure and process that are vital to the development of humanistic skills. The first element in the content of the course is present before training begins, in the experience that the trainees bring to the course. What knowledge needs to be acquired in the training of a humanistic psychotherapist? These are some that are essential for registration:

- the main humanistic theories including a special study one or more methods;
- existential and phenomenological theory;
- some knowledge of the main analytical theories;
- the basics of human development and pathology.

This is a large body of knowledge that could quite easily dominate the training process. It is likely that most humanistic courses attempt to incorporate an integrated approach to psychotherapy, although there is an argument for mastering one method while taking into account other schools. This is particularly true of the body-oriented therapies that require a specialist training. The most important aspect of the content of training is that, within the structure of the course, the individual student has the freedom to pursue what interests or suits him.

One aspect of training that often gets ignored is the danger of exclusiveness if the agency is the sole provider of trainees' experience. One thing I valued about my training in transactional analysis (TA) was the freedom that was encouraged to include half of the required amount hours of training *outside* of the provisions of TA training. I was fortunate in being exposed to a number of teachers who had come into TA from other backgrounds – analysis, bioenergetics, gestalt and social psychiatry.

The other major element of training is what is commonly known as skills practice, in which trainees work in twos or threes or in the group, working with the real problems of their peers, although sometimes it may be necessary to role-play client problems. This has the twofold benefit of focusing on a particular skill or cluster of skills as well as providing an opportunity for ongoing personal growth when acting as the client. By the end of the course, every trainee either finds a placement or has started to see clients on a private basis. Alongside this practical work, the trainee starts the ongoing experience of supervision. Although continuing assessment is essential, there are times, say at the end of terms, when there is a need to have a more formal assessment. At both of these points, there needs to be a joint assessment between the tutor, peers and self. As well as paying particular attention to the course work, the assessments involve whether the trainee understands what is required of him as a potential therapist and if, at a personal level, he is not suitable then he should be invited at least to reconsider whether he should continue. Many people who sign up for a training are seeking to test their vocation – whether they are cut out for this kind of work. It is at this point of reference that future competence is being filtered. If tutors allow trainees to continue when there are major questions about them, then they are storing up trouble for all concerned. This can happen for economic or other reasons, but it has to be watched carefully.

Therapy as part of training

This is another vital aspect of the training experience, which is both for the benefit of the trainee and also for the benefit of future clients in ensuring that he has resolved his major personality issues – something that is regarded as an essential part in the training of the therapist. It is usual that this is undertaken with a therapist experienced in the method that is being studied. It can also be beneficial to have an experience of therapy outside the chosen school and, as I have indicated above, an intensive group experience (which used to be called 'marathons'). Although there is merit in a trainee experiencing therapy in the method in which he is training, I deplore agencies having prescribed lists of suitable practitioners. Although it is not recommended that trainers carry out personal therapy with their trainees, the next worst thing might be forcing trainees into the 'old pals act' for questionable motives. The best way would be to have a minimum of hours in the chosen method and leave the rest for the trainee to choose. Whichever way, the trainee should be free to choose his own therapist – and if that is someone outside the area of his training, all the better.

There is also a danger that the trainee goes into therapy to satisfy the demands of the course rather than from a real connection with his own personal needs. I have known of such people who do therapy in 'term time' and often are not really committed to the process except in some academic way. Worse still, some do not think they have any real issues to work through and go through the motions of the therapeutic process. Fortunately these form a small minority.

So the compulsory nature of undergoing therapy is a mixed blessing. Ideally it is best for it to be voluntary but this would be taking the risk that trainees do not pay attention to their own personal issues. Part of the training is the recognition that therapists need to face a range of issues beyond the realms of personal growth, although it is hoped that they see this as an integration of personal and professional development. Many therapists voluntarily decide to continue their own personal development in a therapeutic context after they have completed their formal training or accreditation.

Chapter 12
Accreditation and competence

Since the turbulence of the early days of the human potential movement there has been a considerable amount of change in the field of humanistic psychotherapy. Not least is the recognition that standards of practice are vital to the maintenance of the work and the protection of clients against incompetence. Gone are the days when an enthusiastic person could go on a short intensive course and start practising because, at that time, there was little recognized training. Now there are dozens of courses that provide accredited training both in counselling and psychotherapy. However, an important question remains: 'how do you measure competence as a humanistic practitioner when there are so many forms?' The range of methodologies, both within humanistic practice and in the field of psychotherapy as a whole, is so wide that lay people must be bewildered in trying to choose a therapist whom they can trust. In his comprehensive survey of counselling and psychotherapy Gerald Corey (1986) seeks to establish criteria for determining competence:

> What is the basis on which practitioners can decide whether they are qualified, or competent, to offer specific professional services? According to the American Psychological Association's *Ethical Standards of Psychologists* (1981): 'Psychologists recognize the boundaries of their competence and the limitations of their techniques and only provide services, use techniques, or offer opinions as professionals that meet recognized standards.' The American Association for Counseling and Development's *Ethical Standards* (1981) state: 'With regard to the delivery of professional services, members should accept only those positions for which they are professionally qualified.' Such a guideline still leaves unanswered the question: 'How can I recognize the boundaries of my competence, and how can I know when I have exceeded them?' This issue is not nearly solved by the mere possession of advanced degrees or of licenses and credentials. In my opinion, many people who complete master's and doctoral programmes in a mental-health speciality still lack the skills needed to effectively function as practitioners. Further, licenses and certification are not necessarily better criteria of competence than degrees. I have encountered some licensed

practitioners who do not appear to possess the competencies specified by their licenses:

Licenses mainly assure the public that the licensees have completed some type of formal academic program, have been exposed to a certain number of hours of supervision, and have completed a minimum number of hours of professional experience . . . Licenses do not, however, assure the public that these practitioners can effectively and competently do what their licenses permit them to do. Further, licenses typically do not specify the types of client or problem the practitioner is competent to deal with or the specialized techniques he or she is skilled in. For example, a licensed psychologist may work very effectively with a certain population of adults yet not be qualified by virtue of training or experience to work with children or adolescents.

The premise is that the public is protected by the setting of minimum standards of service, which is crucial because incompetent practitioners could cause harmful consequences. The literature, however, contains many challenges to the assumption that consumer protection is the intent of licensure. Some suggest that what is being protected is a self-serving guild (Davis, 1981). According to Gross (1978), evidence suggests that existing practices of licensure are so confused that they actually serve to institutionalize a lack of public accountability. He finds no evidence that licensure protects the quality of service rendered, and he contends that the system excludes many competent mental-health professionals. In a similar vein another writer asserts that "the available evidence suggests that the quality of services has not improved since licensing laws have been instituted, disciplinary actions are woefully inadequate, and the prevention of illegal practice is generally spotty and often aimed at eliminating competition, rather than incompetence" (Hogan, 1979, p. 254). And Rogers (1980) has asserted that there are as many certified charlatans as there are uncertified ones. In short, those who challenge professional licensing often maintain that it is designed to create and preserve a 'union shop'. (p. 327)

Two further questions from a humanistic standpoint are 'what is a psychotherapist?' and 'do the norms associated with the title of psychotherapist fit what a humanistic practitioner does?' A person could go to three psychotherapists and have three quite different experiences, from lying on a couch to talking face-to-face in chairs to beating cushions! How can the norms that have been outlined in Part Two of this book be measured?

What has happened is that independent psychotherapists have fallen into two camps: one of self or peer validation and the other through external accreditation. I have described the developments that have taken place in recent years in the UK in Part One. There is no equivalent body to the UKCP, which is a voluntary movement, in most other countries. Registration in many European countries and licensing in North America are controlled by government-appointed bodies. This has resulted in some cases of well-trained and highly qualified professionals being sidelined. In the USA a move to combat this has been the formation of 'associations of life coaches', which avoid the control inherent in the use of the term 'psychotherapist'. Partly this is to enable well-qualified folk to continue to practise and partly it is to counteract the risk of being lumped together with the standards derived from the medical model. So what are the alternatives to licensing and registration?

> One proposal is to replace present licensing practices with a full disclosure by practitioners of information about themselves and about their practice (Gross, 1977; Hogan, 1979). Professional disclosure can take many forms, yet what it comes down to is informing prospective clients about one's qualifications, the nature of the therapeutic process, and important details of the services provided. The rationale is that clients must have this information to make intelligent decisions regarding the use of a practitioner's services. Another alternative is a competency-based model that would entail reviewing specific skills of candidates who apply for entry-level licenses. Further, those who earned a license would be required to demonstrate competent performance at regular intervals as a condition for renewal (Bernstein and Lecomte, 1981). (Corey, 1986, p. 328)

In trying to define what is a *competent* psychotherapist, a resistance to stating what a psychotherapist *is* seems to have developed. The UK Council for Psychotherapy (UKCP) was set up in 1993 with this among its aims. However, there are now more people describing themselves as therapists who are not registered with UKCP. In his controversial book *The Case against Psychotherapy Registration,* Richard Mowbray (1995) clearly sets out the crucial objections and difficulties of any organization seeking to do this. Not the least of his criticisms was the fact that 'the UKCP has established itself without apparently offering a public definition of "psychotherapy", the activity which its seeks to oversee' (p. 52). Unfortunately, in this quest, no one seems to have thought to ask the clients – whatever the practical difficulties of this might be – except through a complaints procedure, which is rather late for the purpose. I say this for two reasons. One is that humanistic psychology avoids such a definition on the common sense basis that if you ask me to taste an apple, I'll be the judge of whether it is an apple or not and if it isn't and I enjoy it, it doesn't matter much. Second, because asking the client is the bedrock of humanistic practice. The therapist invites client to take responsibility for assessing and meeting her own needs. One big step in this direction would be to have, as a matter of course, a form of client assessment every so often. This would involve a lot of extra work but it might worth considering. In addition, some regular method of self/peer assessment would go a long way to ensuring that a therapist in monitoring his work in this way is consciously competent.

Ongoing supervision is an essential part of the continuing training and competence of the therapist. The humanistic approach to psychotherapy does not see the therapist–client relationship in isolation. The therapeutic work consists of an alliance of three, although the third is not physically present in the therapy room. The constant engagement of the therapist with his supervisor forms both a monitoring and supportive presence for the therapist and indirectly for the client. In this respect, it is vital that the relationship of supervisor and therapist is well matched not only in competence but also in sentience. What is to be avoided in this relationship is competitiveness, subservience or one-upmanship. The therapist and the supervisor need to trust each other. There is an implicit authority in the role of the supervisor, who will use this only to ensure protection rather than to act as an overseer or a spy for an external body. There is an exception – when a practitioner has been suspended or put on probation as a result of a complaint and where supervision may be included as part of the sanctions. This is a special case and some would question whether this can be described as 'supervision'. In normal practice the supervisor has no immediate contact with the working life of the therapist, to ensure that their contribution is neutral and uncontaminated by any other interest. There is not the space here to enlarge on this aspect of training and development. Suffice it to say that the quality of the supervision relationship reflects the conditions that apply to humanistic psychotherapy, as noted in Chapter 6.

In their desire to gain greater recognition for their work, many humanistic practitioners have gone along with the assumption that accreditation implies competence. The truth is that, apart from undergoing a recognized form of training by accredited bodies, there are few agreed criteria for competence. It is assumed that the training and accrediting agencies have a monitoring process for measuring this. But how can it be measured? It is important to stress that there is a gap between any means of accreditation and competence. This largely depends on ongoing supervision and training. This may take many different forms – attending conferences and courses, reading and writing, undergoing personal therapy, belonging to a professional body, teaching and training or various extra-curricular activities and life experiences.

In its 2003 handbook, the UK Association for Humanistic Psychology Practitioners (UKAHPP) sets out what is embodied in working humanistically:

> We apply the same criteria of respect, empowerment, authenticity, etc. that we have for our clients, to ourselves personally and professionally. Being humanistic is a way of life, in being committed to one's work and having an awareness of competence, limitations, contextual awareness of social and political concerns and of counter-transferential issues. This necessitates maintaining one's authenticity and having and using a support network that includes supervision and personal and professional development. Although any person can foster self-awareness in another, it requires having humility in relation to others' offerings; knowing we do not have the answers but are fellow searchers; being devoted to self vigilance; being willing to experience vulnerability and uncertainty. (p. 8)

These norms are implicit in both the accreditation process and in the acceptance of them by members of the association. There is also a requirement in this association that every therapist should be engaged in continuing professional development, which is reviewed every five years. Although it is impossible for any system of monitoring to ensure that people practise what they say they do, a greater degree of openness about the way therapists practise would be welcome. At the same time, there is a growing need for more information to be available to the general public. One of the implications for humanistic practice and possibly psychotherapy as a whole is that external regulations not only have a limited effect but could also distract, in the long run, from the real need for psychotherapists to be self-regulatory. This is most likely to be achieved through the careful selection of trainees and the encouragement of openness in the process of training demonstrated by those who train. Then the question is how a practitioner uses supervision and his support network. It is very easy and all too common for newly qualified practitioners to be launched into their work, whether private or in an agency, without a proper regard for how they maintain themselves. Effective agencies insist and ensure that their workers – paid or voluntary – have proper supervision. Many of them pay for it, which is a mixed blessing. Who owns the supervision? Many agencies provide regular group or collegial support. Those who do not have this built-in provision have to look for their own, as indeed do those in private practice. The truth is that no one knows what goes on the therapy session except the therapist and the client. True competence must lie within the critical conscientious of the therapist. In this way the therapist invests his attention in self-supervision. Moreover, the competent therapist will actively seek to sustain his needs through his peers. All training and accrediting organizations should provide opportunities for this. At the same time, all graduates should actively seek a wide range of professional contact. The isolation of being therapists means that they require more than most professionals in this respect.

Chapter 13
The spiritual and the pragmatic

The place of the transpersonal in the practice of humanistic psychotherapy has been a constant tension in humanistic psychology. The humanistic movement could be seen as providing a more realistic alternative to religion in helping people to find their way in their lives. Some would say it has become a kind of religion with its own followers. It is not my purpose to cover the philosophical ideas that lie in the domain of humanistic psychology. This is dealt with by Rowan (2001, Chapter 10), Clarkson (1995, Chapter 6), Jones (1994, Chapters 4–7), Schneider et al. (2001, Chapters 15–16), and Moss (1999, Chapters 11–14). There is also an excellent exposition of transpersonal psychotherapy by Courtenay Young in Chapter 21 later in this book.

What is important in this context is to view the implications of both the humanistic tradition and the beliefs of practitioners. It would be fair to say there is a divide. The divide is between those who assert that only that which is experienced by the five senses is the field of psychotherapy, and those that claim there is more – that human experience includes a spiritual element. Some have profound beliefs that affect their approach to their work with clients. Some adopt a purely pragmatic view of their work. Others recognize that there are aspects of human experience that go beyond the purely physical to what might be described as transcendental. Emerson saw these expressed in justice, beauty, love, goodness and power. That is not to say they do not experience these manifestations in their body. There are many humanistic therapists who have found insight in eastern teachings and practice such as Buddhism, Tantra, Tao, Sufi as well as from the major religions. It has become fairly common for people to use meditation derived from these kind of sources that may open the self to transpersonal contact.

Much of the practice and ideas of the human potential movement were derived from the phenomenological and existential approaches of Perls and Laing. The main thrust that distinguished it from what had gone before was that 'here and now' is the only reality, what is experienced – seen and felt – in the present. This was a move away from a dependence on the supernatural and theory – theological or psychological. At the same time this focus on the physical nature of mankind in the setting of the universe was infused by an acknowledgement of the otherness of life. In his writings, Maslow included 'peak' experiences as elements of the self-actualized person, which transcends individual ego boundaries. Other major thinkers who emphasized the importance of the spiritual were Assagioli (1975), whose model was that the higher self is a mediator between the personality and the divine. Psychosynthesis is the integration of the two. Ken Wilber offers a model in which transpersonal experiences arise from inner developmental structures which are capable of identifying with all levels of the natural environment. Transpersonal psychology became a vector of humanistic psychology, which shares the grounding of ideas in experience. Here again, we experience the contradiction that transpersonal psychology is grounded in experience. Out of this experience people can discover another level, which is part of being fully human.

Paul Tillich, an outstanding theologian of modern times, echoed this connection when he coined the phrase 'the ground of our being'. In a chapter entitled 'The depth of existence', he showed that there are limits to what can be known by natural means:

> Today a new form of this method has become famous, the so-called 'psychology of depth'. It leads us from the surface of our self-knowledge into levels where things are recorded which we knew nothing about on the surface of our consciousness. It shows us traits of character which contradict everything that we believed we knew about ourselves. It can help us to find the way into our depth, although it cannot help us in an ultimate way, because it cannot guide us to deepest ground of our being and of all being, the depth of life itself.
>
> The name of this infinite and inexhaustible depth and ground of all being is *God*. That depth is what the word *God* means. And if that word has not much meaning for you, translate it, and speak of the depths of your life, of the source of your being, of your ultimate concern, of what you take seriously without any reservation. (Paul Tillich, 1948)

How does this apply to the practice of humanistic psychotherapy? What effect does a belief in God, or a higher being, have on the way that therapy is conducted? It can help to make sense of irrational or tragic experience. On the other hand it can get in the way of seeing clearly what is there and making it into something you believe is there. Having a Christian background myself, I found it was one thing I didn't want to bring consciously into therapy. There is enough to deal with in the therapeutic process without having to wonder what this might mean at another level, which can be only deduced or presumed or at worst interpreted.

If a practitioner calls himself a transpersonal therapist, then it is clear to anyone who seeks his help what he is offering. If he has beliefs and practices, not only must he respect anyone else's beliefs or non-beliefs, but ensure that he is not overtly or subtlety influencing his clients to take on his beliefs. On the other hand, if people come to him with their own experiences and beliefs, religious or otherwise, the fact that he has a comparable experience or belief system may assist him empathizing with them: '. . . transpersonal therapists assume that one goal of therapy is to facilitate growth of the self toward these higher levels of experience' (Hastings/Moss, 1999, p. 203). That is fine provided that their clients want to achieve 'enlightenment'. It is incumbent upon those who practise humanistic therapy to keep their feet on the ground and stay in close touch with where their clients are. It is not my business here to have an intellectual discussion about what is real or what is the truth. God only knows! I am dealing here with the implications of different beliefs on practice.

Some transpersonal therapists would not include themselves in the humanistic camp. They see it as a separate discipline – a 'fourth force'. However, in the *Handbook of Humanistic Psychology* (Schneider et al., 2001), David Elkins (pp. 201–11) points out that the transpersonal has always played a part in the (American) Association of Humanistic Psychology from Maslow, the founder, onward. The *Journal of Humanistic Psychology* publishes articles on transpersonal themes. There have been both theoretical and organizational disputes but these 'are generally supportive'.

What is the relation of humanistic principles to religion? This is a different question to the spiritual nature of much of what traditionally humanistic psychology has espoused. It is true that many of the originators of humanistic therapy, from Carl Rogers to Frank Lake, had their roots in some religious upbringing or belief. Many of those who found new inspiration in the humanistic movement were people of some religious persuasion who had been disillusioned by their own faith and found freedom to express what they truly believed about life and people without all the encumbrances of institutional religion. This was particularly true of the American west coast where many derived their inspiration from Eastern awakenings, which were a secular religion that affected people like Perls, Schutz and Swartley. When humanistic beliefs and principles are examined, they can be recognized as having similar values related to human existence as the major religions. It would be impossible for me to speak for religion in general, but there is a close resemblance between humanistic beliefs and the Christian ethic 'love thy neighbour as thyself'.

Chapter 14
Contact and boundaries

Writing this section proved to be the most demanding part of the book because I recognize that, although this is the heart of the humanistic approach, it is the most exacting to put into words without falling into over-subjectivity or over-principled statements. Anyone who has faced these issues squarely will understand the dilemma. In this, I have drawn upon Kottler (1990) and Yalom (1989) whose works are well worth reading to explore these issues further and discover one's own resolution. Finding a balance between caring for clients and staying separate is the biggest challenge for the humanistic therapist, requiring both skill and awareness. This balance is the key for effective relationships. Although there are codes of practice within which most practitioners work, each client and each situation determines what is most acceptable for both parties.

So what are the issues here for humanistic therapy? Clearly our motto, in common with all who are in the helping professions, must be 'do no harm'. The most common need for clients coming into therapy is that of gaining trust in relationships. Many have not experienced a close relationship, or have experienced only painful ones. The nature of the relationship in humanistic therapy is one that encourages openness and trust. The therapist is willing to be transparent and own his own part in the relationship. However, if any significant change is going to take place in the client, she will make an attachment to the therapist and vice versa. The therapist will accept this but will respond with respectful appropriateness. There is a possibility that the client will become unduly dependent on the therapist.

Clearly therapy has risks – indeed, in order for the client to grow there needs to be an element of risk. The therapist is there to encourage the client to step out of her safe, if uncomfortable, place into what will be a more rewarding way of relating. It is in the nature of intimate relationships to take risks. What the humanistic therapist is aiming to do is to demonstrate not how to avoid pain but how not to let the risk and experience of hurt prevent a healing outcome. The essence of a humanistic therapeutic relationship is to share in a process in which both people have and experience their power. In this, both experience the risks involved in intimacy. Our clients do have an effect on us:

> Great wracking sobs could be heard through the door, not an unusual occurrence in a psychiatric clinic except that the client had left five minutes earlier. Only the therapist remained – alone, behind the door. Tears streamed down his face. He was huddled in a ball on the floor. The therapist had been conducting a particularly intense session with a man who was mourning the loss of his unborn son. As he was helping the client accept the miscarriage and find hope in the future he realized at some point he was no longer speaking to the client but to himself. His own girlfriend had decided, upon ending their relationship, to unceremoniously abort their baby. The therapist had long ago worked through his loss, the pain, and the disappointment. Yet, it all came tumbling forth again as his client struggled with a similar issue. Against all restraint, all objectivity, all desire to help the client, he lost the separateness between himself and the other. (Kottler, 1990, p. 9)

There is also a risk that the therapist will become involved in a way that hinders the therapeutic process and may adversely affect his own sense of himself. This may be to meet his own needs beyond the limits of the therapeutic relationship, which may possibly stem from his desire to be there for the client. We are involved with and affected by our clients, no matter how separate we remain. Not to acknowledge this is a denial of the human condition and the nature of therapeutic activity. Much of this has satisfying outcomes. Some of this has a negative effect. Hopefully, the humanistic therapist acknowledges this and takes it into account and uses his supervision and support to correct the balance.

One of the aims of humanistic therapy is to create an environment where there is a recognition of essential equality. 'Since therapists, no less than patients, must confront the givens of existence, the professional posture of disinterested objectivity . . . is inappropriate. We are . . . in this together' (Yalom, 1980, p. 14). Yalom believes that personal concealment denies the client the opportunity to experience a more genuine, loving encounter (Kottler, 1990, p. 37):

> This encounter, the very heart of psychotherapy, is a caring, deeply human meeting between two people, one (generally, but not always, the patient) more troubled than the other. Therapists have a dual role . . . As observer, one must be sufficiently objective to provide necessary rudimentary guidance to the patient. As participant, one enters into the life of the patient and is affected and sometimes changed by the encounter. (Yalom, 1980, p.13)

It is easy to fall into the narcissistic trap of control to avoid involvement. 'We can distance ourselves from pain by retreating inside our chairside manner – a delusion that we have the power to heal . . . To give up our narcissistic stance is to risk a deeper, more terrifying form of self-involvement: to confront the feelings we fear most' (Kottler, 1990, p. 54). Transference can be a veil to hide the unease. It is unrealistic and unreasonable to think about total detachment in therapy or to imagine that one person in this setting is without problems or needs.

Humanistic therapists regard emotional contact with clients as a vital part of the process. Many have a genuine affection for their clients, but it is more than just a natural liking; it is a result of developing a disciplined positive attitude to people. This emotional connection is to be feared only by those who do not have a strong emotional sense of themselves. The therapist recognizes his part in the relationship as being valid. There is a mutual need for the therapeutic relationship at a number of levels. There is, of course, some level of mutual dependency in all relationships. In personal relationships this can be beneficial or misused. In professional relationships, whether they involve plumbers or solicitors, this can be legitimate or used to defraud. In the helping professions, where the service offered is personal and depends on trust, this is even more open to risk. Often this is an integral part of the process. So it is essential to have safeguards – such as making clear contracts, keeping within acceptable boundaries and showing respect for the stated needs of the client.

However, it is not quite as simple as that. For example, in any work situation it is clear that the task is paramount. Good working relationships are also important, not only in carrying out the task but in ensuring that people are engaged in an enterprise that brings an intrinsic sense of wellbeing. It is true that people do make social contacts in the workplace. Dating is common. Using the firm's e-mail facility for this purpose is an everyday occurrence but no one would give that behaviour unqualified consent. It is also a fact that the large majority of people find their partners, temporary or permanent, in their working situation. This means that a large amount of energy is exercised outside the overt purpose of the organization. Without pushing this analogy to its limits, the main point is that both are working situations and the question is 'does this extra curricular activity undermine the given purpose?'

Coming back to the therapy consulting room, this is also a place of work. Here, it is likely to undermine the purpose of the relationship. The work is the facilitation of the clients' healing and therefore the clients' interests are paramount, not to the exclusion of the therapists' interest. They not only have a responsibility for maintaining a safe environment, they also need to keep clear of going beyond what is in the interests of their clients and to find a way of maintaining themselves in the process. Most therapists exercise great care in maintaining clear boundaries.

The whole business depends on finding a healthy balance. What does this mean? The therapist does not take unfair advantage of the vulnerability of the client. The therapist watches his own vulnerability to ensure that he does not use his clients to minister to his emotional lacking or to blur his own sense of responsibility. This does not mean that he has to be superior. To admit his limitations, to express his feelings, may be helpful and liberating for his clients and encourage them to take responsibility for themselves. At the same time he must be on guard for anything in himself or his clients that may lead to any temptation to cross the line of good manners, etiquette and common decency.

In finding the best balance between making contact and maintaining good boundaries, we need to examine how contact is made. The means whereby therapists and clients achieve their agreed aim is varied. Some do it verbally sitting face to face – listening, asking questions; some do it through physical expression or manipulation; some do it lying on their back with the therapist out of sight. Whatever the method, there are areas that are considered out of bounds for the therapist: physical contact with ulterior motives; social contact outside the therapy room; business or financial involvement; using information for covert purposes without the knowledge of the client; and using the trust of the client in a professional relationship for self-serving ends that have nothing to do with the therapy.

These come under the heading of what has become known as 'dual relationships' – where contact is made in two differing settings, where the roles may change and the relationship is not clear. There is plenty of evidence that this can lead to unnecessary problems. Apart from the ethical dilemmas that may arise, most practitioners avoid dual relationships with their clients to avoid complications. There has been some discussion supporting dual relationships, showing that it is often not possible or necessarily helpful to avoid them – for example, to see the therapist in another setting can sometimes help the client to see him as an ordinary person.

The *Transactional Analysis Journal,* volume 24, number 1, contained a number of articles on dual relationships, which pointed out both their risks and their unavoidability. While saying that we should avoid any misuse of such relationships, the articles also warned against the overly legalistic attitude that can result in 'defensive' therapy – overly concerned with avoiding mistakes.

As soon as you attend training or therapy workshops, it is likely either you will meet your therapist, client, supervisor or trainer. There is no way you can make rules about this – each person will handle each situation as best he can and he may make a mistake. Making a mistake, we are taught, is a way of learning. In July 2001 the Humanistic and Integrative Psychotherapy Section (HIPS) of UKCP (2001) implemented a six-page policy statement on dual relationships that seems to be negative and unduly detailed. It seems that the longer therapy is a profession, the longer the rules get.

Now it is an accepted norm that the therapist does not have relationships with his clients outside the clear boundaries of the session, but under what circumstances are these potentially harmful, harmless or possibly beneficial? Here are a few examples.

- A female client said to her therapist 'You are my best friend and I would love you to come home with me.' He replied 'Although I like you, I am not your friend, I am your therapist.'
- A male client invited his therapist to a wine tasting. 'No I can't, I am busy.'
- A man expressed his wish to join him for a beer to end therapy. 'Fine. I'd like that too.'
- An attractive woman kept asking her therapist personal questions. He answered them straightforwardly at the time and then she never asked again.
- The mother of a teenage client asked if the therapist would house her wayward son. He agreed and they worked out a clear contract that allowed the son a breathing space and improved his relationship with his parents.

I make no comment about these cases, but leave it to readers to draw their own conclusions, which might be different because it is not only the 'facts' that are relevant but also the persons involved and so many variable factors in any given situation. Hopefully, most of our training and experience as well as our intuition will help us to make the best decisions. All professionals recognize the need for boundaries. When I go to my hairdresser, I don't expect to be helping him with his personal problems, although that is one of the risks of our profession. I remember one of my colleagues avoided this, when strangers asked him what his job was, by telling them he was a private detective (which wasn't that far from the truth). That soon stopped any intrusion!

Chapter 7 outlines a profile of a humanistic therapist as a person having his own life in some sort of order and balance. This pre-empts the unnecessary invasion by his clients. How do you decide what is intrusive? What part of the therapist's life is no business of his clients and has no place in the therapeutic environment? Does it matter whether your clients know whether or not you are married or have children or have certain leisure activities, and so forth? There can be no ultimate answer to these considerations. Some therapists want to remain anonymous. Some don't. Some clients are interested in what sort of a person you are outside of the sessions. Some could not care less or find that area irrelevant or would rather not know. A question that must be asked is whether therapists merely keep personal information to themselves, and maybe their supervisors, or do they convey this in some way to their clients, directly or indirectly. Our clients know a lot more about us than we sometimes imagine. There may be a range of opinion with the humanistic community about this. While acknowledging the vital aspects of humanistic therapy are that of transparency, congruence and integrity, there would be many interpretations of how this is manifested.

We are trained to restrain our natural impulses and yet are encouraged to show empathy, to be genuine but not to say too much about ourselves.

Here is another one of those contradictions with which therapists have to live. Being humanistic therapists means we have to tread a narrow path between being ourselves and being for the client by depriving ourselves.

I have discussed, above, the issue of self-disclosure and the nature of the therapist's investment in his clients. What about the needs of the therapist? How are the needs of the therapist legitimately met in the therapeutic relationship? Kottler talks about the healing of the therapist in his work (1990, p. 28). Not only are we challenged by our clients' lives and struggles – we are also changed by the way we have to confront our own 'dis-ease', which is stimulated by our clients' problems. We are also nourished by the contact with them. On the other hand, Henri Nouwen wrote a book called *The Wounded Healer* (1994) in which he asserted that it is through their weakness that healers are strong enough to bear the pain of others, but they should avoid using their work for their own healing (pp. 87–8).

Although there are clear guidelines for professional practice, they touch only a fraction of the dilemmas that therapists have to face daily. It is probable that most experienced therapists have a highly developed sense of intuition that guides them through the troubled waters of their practice. But what happens when the therapist is genuinely in doubt? For example, a client came to live in the same street as her therapist. Should he ask her to end therapy? How should he greet her outside?

In the UK Association of Humanistic Practitioners (UKAHPP) there is a facility open to its members called an ethical review, through which a practitioner can check with his colleagues how to handle a difficult situation. Although in theory this is a valuable resource, the truth is that this procedure is very rarely used. So it could be contended that, with all the codes and guidelines, in the end it comes down to each individual therapist working though the complications for himself and hopefully avoiding any misuse of the client's trust. This is all very well but, of course, this does not always work and therapists can cross the line either accidentally or knowingly. Then we move into the arena of complaints. There are very few of these, so it could be assumed that a lot of things go wrong that never come to light. This may in some cases be the best thing, to avoid any further problems for the client, although this is regrettable. Aware of this difficulty, the UKAHPP has a policy of mediation prior to any formal complaint, which provides the opportunity for some remedial work in a safe environment.

Although there is much attention given to the risks for the client when things go wrong (there is a complaints procedure that they can pursue), not enough consideration is given to the risks for the therapist. For example, therapists are bound by a rule of confidentiality; clients are not. It is not easy for a client to choose to instigate a complaint. It is also not easy for the therapist. It is probable that most boundary issues are and can be avoided by encouraging a spirit of openness in the sessions, but there is no guarantee.

Now for the most part, in this section, I have dealt with the difficulties in making contact and setting boundaries. What underlies all that has been said is the purpose of humanistic therapy, which is to engage in an authentic relationship with clients – to care for the client and to be as honest and open as possible. We give of ourselves in this and our clients give a lot of themselves too. We often become close, sometimes closer than with our friends. We share strong feelings in the relationship and this can lead us into a mutual delusion of friendship or more. In some cases it can involve sexual feelings.

The forbidden zone

The most outstanding boundary issue seems to be about inappropriate sex between the therapist and client. But it is important to recognize that there are other areas that are less obvious but potentially just as offensive and harmful – for example, overcharging; providing a service that a practitioner is unqualified to offer; maintaining a therapeutic relationship when it is not in the interests of the client; letting clients leave when they are unprotected; working with a person with whom the therapist has a conflicting interest; or using the relationship as a means of furthering the therapist's own ambitions.

However, it is the area of breaking sexual boundaries that Peter Rutter (1989) called the 'forbidden zone' and that attracts a lot more attention than any other in all professional relationships. Although proceedings against malpractice seem to have become common in the actual treatment of patients in the health service and clients elsewhere, this word does not seem to be used much in psychotherapy. It is the breaking of trust caused by sexual relationships that seems to be the source of much damage.

In the early days of the growth movement, all norms of behaviour and thinking were being questioned – not the least in the area of sexuality. It was in a social climate where free love was being practised and open marriage was being heralded as a model for honest relationships. Marriage, fidelity and any establishment rules were disputed. Some anarchists believed that the establishment needed to collapse before true freedom would come. There was a magazine called *Oz* that was an outspoken vehicle of this movement. One of its targets was the institution of marriage as the main bulwark of the establishment. No doubt this was a necessary rebellion against hypocrisy and oppressive restrictions, particularly for the young. Wilhelm Reich (1951) wrote that 'Chastity . . . creates the conditions which, though not intended by the existing social order, are inevitably part of its sexual regime . . . monogamous marriage gives rise to *adultery,* and the chastity of girls to *prostitution*' (p. 35).

In the field of therapy this was also being acted out. There were a number of charismatic leaders who made it clear that everyone they worked with must take responsibility for themselves and they were unwilling to conform to the usual sexual norms. Sexual mores were seen as an obstacle to personal freedom. In an adjacent arena of communes, free love was the norm. However, away from the excesses of these 'no-limits' encounter-type groups, these experiments were in the minority, and the majority of practitioners condemned them as abusive. However, because they received a lot of publicity, the general public saw these practices as scary and offputting, which led to a certain amount of distrust in groups.

Therapy has moved a long way from those early days and voluntarily imposed censure on any behaviour that breaks the sexual boundary between practitioner and client. As a result of increasing sanctions, many therapists are now cautious about touching their clients, as much for their own protection as that of their clients. This may be the safest policy but many recognize that the client may be the loser. How is this issue dealt with in body-orientated therapies where physical contact is the norm? Here the boundary issues need to be even more carefully monitored. Physical contact, however, is still regarded as an integral part of humanistic therapy by many practitioners. There are times when touching is just what is needed. It can be used appropriately and with consent. It is possible to give a hug without it being misconstrued.

In this sensitive area the therapist faces a number of contradictions. The dilemma is that if humanistic therapists are to be fully human and be themselves with their clients, then part of their humanity is their sexuality. Can this be expressed without being seductive? Clearly, the therapist is not there to seduce clients. It is important to acknowledge that clients can use their sexuality to manipulate the therapist. The other important fact is that this is a risk for both female and male therapists. Flirtation can be a way to divert the process of therapeutic relationship. Confronting this can lead to further confusion.

Most complaints about sexual misconduct are brought against male therapists. It is hard to recall a woman being brought up on an ethics charge. Is that because it doesn't happen? I doubt it. It is more likely because few men would have the courage or wish to accuse a woman therapist. It is also interesting to note that, for the best of reasons, therapists cannot bring an ethics charge against clients, however offensive they may be. It is assumed that therapists are strong enough and experienced enough to deal with this without any harm to them.

There is an element that seems bent on sanitizing the therapist's sexual feelings. In a handbook of innovative therapy, Jones (1994, p. 217) stated that indulging in sexual fantasies and daydreams about clients is abusive. While this is intended to be cautionary it seems to be pushing the boundaries a bit far and being unrealistically over-protective. For whom, one may wonder. It cannot be that a 'Persil-white' approach to therapy helps in dealing with the realities of life and our human condition.

The possible consequences of deep emotional or sexual involvement between therapist and client are just too difficult for both parties to manage. Being a therapist is hard enough without all that complication. Being in therapy takes a lot out of the client. If the client becomes too attached to the therapist, or vice versa, then that will be a distraction. The therapist needs to be careful and to have the stability to avoid entanglement. For this reason, therapists maintain the standards of the profession both in the interests of their clients and equally for their own protection. Nevertheless, the erotic will always be an element in the work. 'Erotic love, if it is love, has one premise. That I love from the essence of my being – and experience the other person in the essence of his or her being . . . To love somebody is not *just* a strong feeling – it is a decision' (Fromm, 1962, p. 44). This is true of any relationship, including the therapeutic relationship.

> To ignore the far-reaching, powerfully violent and seductive forces of love and erotic attraction available out of awareness in the consulting room is potentially to limit beyond tolerance what clients can expect to have from their therapy. On the other hand I believe it is essential to consider the implications of the fact that some form of betrayal of the primal trust (Hillman, 1975b) is an essential part of existential and personal maturation and that it is as important for the therapist not to provide a false, Utopian, secure haven from the vicissitudes of real life. Winnicott and Kohut always draw attention to the importance of 'failure' on the part of the therapist. This does not mean intentional evil-doing – merely the recognition that in the humanity of the physician there are many flaws – not all to the detriment of the patient. The most effective work may lie in the interstices of working through these failures rather than in the promise or provision of 'holding' in some womb-like Utopia – which means nowhere. (Clarkson, 1995, p. 310)

Ideas, rules and theories do not touch the basic issue, which is summarized in the norm that clients may be encouraged to reveal their secrets in a one-way intimacy but therapists are not supposed to do that, for very good reasons no doubt. It was hoped that one of the prevailing conditions of therapy prior to the growth movement – that we are all at the mercy of primitive forces – was challenged by a more benevolent view of human beings. We believe that sexuality is one of the best gifts of life; we support, encourage and accept the sexual feelings of our clients even when they are directed, welcome or unwelcome, at us. But that is one thing we do not seem to allow for ourselves, even though we may acknowledge that it affects us in the therapeutic relationship one way or another. 'Only when we are willing to identify and explore how we feel about our clients and how it affects our clinical judgement can we ever hope to harness this energy constructively' (Kottler, 1990, p. 71).

Chapter 15
Feelings and love

Invariably what brings people into therapy is that they are feeling bad. These feelings, as Claude Steiner (1975) pointed out, are due to a lack of love, joy, power or thought. One of the liberations of the humanistic movement was that it gave people permission to feel – to have their feelings, value their feelings, express their feelings. I remember the title of a book called *Free to Feel* by Jerome Liss (1974) in which he covered the breadth of the new therapies and how they helped people out of the constrictions of a non-feeling culture through groups, communities, body therapies and co-counselling. The basic feelings of gladness, sadness, anger and fear are essential not only for human survival but also for personal growth. They are the signalling system integrated into the body to tell us when something needs attention; parallel to physical discomfort.

It is not the purpose of this book to expound too much on theory. In this instance it can take us away from the experience. Perls' message 'Get out of your head and come to your senses' is needed, to see and hear clearly as well as to be aware of what we are doing with ourselves. The way in which we have coped with our physical sensations through life gives rise to how we feel, and dealing with feelings is at the heart of humanistic psychotherapy. To help people get release from the prohibitive parental injunctions that say 'don't have the feelings you are having'. One of the major contributions of most forms of humanistic practice is that it gives a place for people to come to let their feelings out. Although some people are expressive with their feelings, most have difficulty with some type of feeling. It is one of the main tasks of the humanistic therapist not only to support clients in their feelings but also to find better ways of using them, whether they are rational or not. Anyway, what is a rational feeling (another contradiction) – justifiable, appropriate, relevant, acceptable? All these are thoughts that need to be taken into account, but only after the event of having and or expressing them. One of the constant questions asked of clients is 'what are you feeling?' The therapist asserts that it is OK for them to be sad, angry, scared or hilarious. It is just as important for the therapist to encourage feelings like satisfaction, amusement, enjoyment as well as those that are painful.

As has already been noted, the clients' expression of feelings can have an effect on the therapist. The therapist also brings his own legitimate feelings, some of which belong to him and have nothing to do with the client, except that if the therapist is going through a hard time or having a wonderful time this might impinge to some extent on the client, unless the therapist is 'buttoned up'. The client, too, has feelings, positive or negative, about the therapist. How does the therapist respond? When is it OK for the therapist to disclose his feelings about the client or what is going on in the session or, for that matter, about what is going on in his life? Whatever the answer to these questions, the therapist's agenda is not to be used to dominate the relationship.

In the therapeutic setting, just as elsewhere, love can be diminished by dismissing it as dependency, transference, obsession, infatuation, passion, eroticism regarding these as having nothing to do with love. How do we know love but through attraction (filial, sexual or erotic), affection, regard, admiration, respect, care? It is bound to be experienced in one of these forms. It may not be 'pure love', if there is such a thing. Love, of course, is more than feeling, although it is always involves a feeling. Love in one form or another is at the core of all fulfilling relationships and this is no less or more true of the therapeutic relationship. Without love, therapy is merely a function, a service.

Love is the feeling experience a person has inside himself about another that has a special value. There can be no more clear expression of this than that written by Erich Fromm (1962). It is, as he says, an art that has many different forms and expressions. 'Love is the active concern for the life and growth of that which we love' (p. 23). There could not be a better description of the nature of humanistic therapy.

PART FOUR
SIX VIEWS OF HUMANISTIC PSYCHOTHERAPY

The following chapters comprise six accounts by psychotherapists with differing methods of working from a humanistic standpoint. They do not claim to be representative of a school. They have been invited to describe how their work is humanistic as individual therapists. As you will observe, their contributions are varied and their styles diverse. This is to show the inclusive nature of the humanistic approach while retaining, to a greater or lesser extent, their concurrence with the core beliefs and principles. They represent only a portion of the work that might be included, but nevertheless give the reader some idea of the widespread nature of this approach. I make no comments on what they have written. Their words speak for themselves.

Chapter 16
To work in this way is a blessing

JULIE ANNE HEWSON

To begin at the beginning:
A Blessing:
Blessed be the longing that brought you here and that quickens your soul with wonder.
May you have the courage to befriend your eternal longing.
May you enjoy the critical and creative companionship of the question 'Who am I?' and may it brighten your longing.
May a secret providence guide your thought and shelter your feelings.
May your mind inhabit your life with the same sureness with which your body belongs in the world.
May the sense of something absent enlarge your life.
May your soul be as free as the ever new waves of the sea.
May you succumb to the danger of growth.
May you live in the neighbourhood of wonder.
May you belong to love with the wildness of dance.
May you know that you are ever embraced in the kind circle of God.

John O'Donohue (1998)

As I sat to start writing this chapter, after thinking about it for some considerable time, on how I work, humanistically from an integrative/ transactional analytic approach, I felt I had to begin at the beginning with a blessing.

Recently, in Exeter, a new Café Internet base has been set up by two men and their families, one from Libya and the other from Palestine. What touched me was the motivation behind this new venture. It was to provide a safe base for visiting students from the Middle East to the university, providing familiar food, contact with others from the same areas and ensuring safe arrivals, including being met from the airport and being found accommodation. A sceptic might have another take on it, in this current fearful climate, but their welcome to us (many of my students go there now) and the courtesy as well as pain in the current situation in the Middle East, showed many of the principles that I associate with the best of humanistic philosophy, 'freedom, dignity, individuation and growth' (Wahl, 2001). Above all, they began and ended our encounters with a blessing, and I remembered how it has always been such in Celtic society too.

Our work in psychotherapy is to me a blessing in the widest sense of the word. It has been described as 'entering as a partner into a person-to-person relationship, never through the observation and investigation of an object' (Bragan, 1996, p. 10), referring to Buber's approach in the 'I–thouness' of relationship, and Kohut who talks of the 'ambience of sustained empathic resonance'. Relationship is at the core of my work, with individual people, groups and organizations and teams in difficulty. Fractured relationships with oneself and others are, in my opinion, the cause of many of the woes and worries enacted in this paradoxical world of ours. They lead to fear that there is not enough to go round, that others must give perfect mirroring otherwise all is lost, that being understood is more important than understanding, that all conflict is bad, that we are separate and individualistic at the cost of acknowledging that everything we think and do will impact on each other because of the interconnectedness of all things. People look for certainty and are faced with chaos, people look for creativity and are forced into structures, somehow we have to hold the beliefs in the innate value of all human beings and I would say life itself, whilst acknowledging the destructive and random annihilation of people, property, societies and natural environments. How are we to determine what is our responsibility and what it is we have to live through and with others, where there seems no rhyme or reason for the events encountered?

How do I reconcile some of these beliefs and paradoxes with integrative psychotherapy and a transactional analytic approach? When I first encountered transactional analysis I had been recommended by a colleague to investigate it, as a lecturer in academic psychology, and having begun my personal journey on a transpersonal path. I was quite hostile to the idea, I remember, as, from what I had heard, I found the language gauche and the concepts apparently over-simplistic. What I discovered to my surprise was that many of the schools of psychology I had been studying and teaching were represented in this surprisingly integrating model. I also discovered I could translate into English, concepts that had originally been designed to make complex ideas accessible to a particular American client group in the 1950s and 1960s. One humorous discovery was the term *racket*, in relation to inauthentic or substitute feelings. When I first heard the term I though it related to tennis, being a British subject, encountering it as I did, for the first time during the Wimbledon fortnight. I later discovered that it related to the American concept of the 'protection racket' based on the activities of Al Capone, with whom Berne's original clients would have been very familiar.

As with all intuitive people, I have always needed to make sense of, or create meaning from, what I have heard, seen and felt. In my relationship with clients I began to notice early on that I was responding with all of me to their story and the way they presented themselves. As with any beginning practitioner, I found myself moving in and out of the observer role, noticing how moved or not moved I was, allowing full rein to my curiosity, in the service of endeavouring to understand the client's frame of reference and view of the world, and also noticing my own empathic attunement to the often well-hidden core of the person. Transactional analysis gave me some frames in which to couch the unspoken 'I wonder'. In fact the word 'wonder' has become central to my thinking as I am often filled with wonder at the resilience, creativity and ingenuity of the human spirit in adversity.

Eric Berne was an outsider, epitomizing the Observer archetype, clever, astute, rather emotionally awkward but a keen noticer of patterns. His legacy was an incredible ability to ask about the significance of such patterns. Why would someone like this have to behave in this way in order to survive?

What is the significance of these external ways of relating to the expression of the client's inner dialogue?

Transactional analysis (TA) is based on a number of traditions of psychological knowledge and philosophical influences. It is a theory based originally on psychoanalytic concepts and psychodynamic awareness, and further influenced by the object relations development in Britain. It also demonstrates a clear acknowledgement of developmental psychology, existential principles, and learning theory. It was strongly influenced by the humanistic ideas, the *zeitgeist* of the 1960s in the USA. What has become clear over the past 10 years is that it has been impacted by the rise in the influence of self-psychology, both in the methodology as well as conceptual framework of modern transactional analytic thinking.

How has all this influenced my work?

To begin with, I would say that transactional analysis, as an integrating approach, gave me permission to use the whole of me in relationship. I could use my personal response as information; I could notice how I was moved or left unaffected, I could consider whether this response was of my own personal history or the result of unconscious processes on the part of the client wishing to invite me into a familiar transferential role. I could use my awareness of any incongruity between what was said and how it was said. I could notice redefining transactions. I could notice the images and metaphors that came about as the relationship developed. I could notice what emerged between us, and above all I could notice the essential worth of the person in front of me, their struggle for understanding, repair, acceptance, deconfusion and contact. I could also notice at what age the person in trauma or distress was fixated.

As I write these words, the reader might notice the language of gestalt, core process, self-psychology, developmental, humanistic and transactional analysis being used alongside one another. Gestalt and TA have always worked well together, and increasingly the awareness of self psychology and the significance of the early rupture to contact, has led to the clear development of an integratively/relationally based school of transactional analysis to join the other existing three. What is important is that integration works in the service of the client, that no one approach has all the answers, a point very well discussed by Wahl (2001), where he reflects on the different universes of discourse each approach can represent.

Integrative transactional analytic frameworks give me a way of considering a range of factors in relating. These include the healing dialogue, where through the awareness of the eight needs in relationship (Erskine et al., 1999) I as therapist can calibrate the perceived reparative need alongside well-understood normal human relational needs. These ideas go beyond the original core conditions of Rogers (1951), which were quite revolutionary against the backdrop of the then 'therapeutic landscape' (Erskine et al., 1999, p. 1). These eight needs are taken from various writers from the realm of self psychology with whom Rogers himself would have been familiar, especially Kohut, Masterson and Wolff, and include the following:

1. *The need for security* (merger transference), bonding and being accepted for who I am, the fostering of a deep sense of security, feeling 'I am OK you are OK'. The therapist needs to attune to developmental needs, affect and rhythm and create acts of security.
2. *The need to feel affirmed and validated* (mirroring transference), to be acknowledged, to be treated as significant. Feelings and needs will need affirming and validation. Failure to validate inner life or proceeding too quickly can lead to juxtaposition.
3. *The need to be accepted by a stable, dependable reliable other.* The question: is there someone out there strong enough to protect me from my own intrapsychic punishment? Therapists need to behave consistently and reliably and keep contracts.
4. *The need to have their experience validated.* When this need arises the client may need to feel in the presence of someone similar, and ask, 'how is my therapist like me?' Twinship transference, creating a common philosophy reciprocity and joy, learning and growing together from the experience.
5. *The need to define oneself and feel unique and still be supported without humiliation and rejection* (adversarial transference). This need signifies the clients' quests to be supported in their uniqueness, their individuation and separation. The client will need support and encouragement in defining and being responsible for self. The relationship is one where the client can say 'no' and still stay in contact a lot of the time.
6. *The need to make an impact on the other.* Here the client has an enhanced sense of self and personal efficacy. Our will is taken seriously by the other and there is an increasing sense of competence of contact in the relationship.

7. *The need to have the other initiate.* This is profoundly important for children who reached out and always had to initiate contact; it is a great healing when the therapist reaches out to them.
8. *The need to love and give, to be grateful.* People do need to thank and be glad for receiving. This has been somewhat pathologized in psycho-analytic literature. It is a normal human need.

In addition, the work of Daniel Stern has had a profound influence on the fine-tuning of relationships, especially when early contact has been frac-tured.

These ideas help with the notion of complex relatedness, which is the essence of the therapeutic encounter. The 'thereness' (Josselson, 1996. p. 31), the eye-to-eye validation (Josselson, 1996, p. 111) and the possibility of more evenness of emotional supplies. These themes and ideas all con-tribute to the humanistic view, which are summed up by Whitton (1992) as being based on the premiss that 'knowledge of oneself, of others and of the world is based essentially on inner experience' and that the approach is thus one of 'experiential encounter'. Therefore, anything that adds to knowledge and understanding or that can expand our inner expe-rience is surely all to the good. This, for me, includes a knowledge and appreciation of literature from beyond these shores, art, music, religion and culture. To be a resourced therapeutic companion we owe it to those who seek our help to keep expanding our understanding of the human condition through dialogue, through film, through travel, through being willing to learn from all encounters. Whitton talks of the theory of human nature, the aims of growth and therapy, the nature of the therapeutic rela-tionship, and from these key concepts expands on the core aspects of humanistic practice. I would have little difficulty in subscribing to all of these principles of practice, and in addition would add that we are all energy and the therapeutic encounter is an exchange of energy. The stuck energy or fixated states or stuck patterns of repetition compulsion (ego-states and games, respectively, in transactional analytic parlance) can equally well be described as historical thought fields that no longer rep-resent the current reality and the subsequent re-enactment of that subjective reality. Current work in energy psychology and meridian-based therapies can also be integrated into a humanistic way of working where the relationship is paramount.

I shall return to this later in the chapter.

In his book *Self and Spirit, the Therapeutic Relationship*, Bragan (1996) draws attention to the fact that, since the seventeenth century, 'There has been a major shift from internal to external discourse' and, referring to George Steiner, a commentator on literature and language, goes on to say:

and he [George Steiner] gives this a special significance because 'the in-ternal modes of self address may enact absolutely primary and indispensable functions of identity.' On the basis of this the hypothesis is offered, that this shift to external discourse from the internal may be a large part responsible for alienation and anomie, rather than simply attributing it to economics and politics. With the rise of reflective practice in a number of professional fields, the chance to explore our inner response to external pressures is becoming increasingly acknowledged as essential for good practice and psychological balance and integration. The need for 'quiet time and self collection' is part of the business of psychotherapy, a time for 'self restoration'. (Bragan, 1996, p. 13)

So having established the importance of the relationship, the value and dignity of the person, how can I help clients to be aware of their ability to choose and change?

In the body of knowledge of transactional analysis there are some very useful ideas that, when shared with the client, can normalize and celebrate the client's creativity in choice making. One of these concepts is that of the script. It has been defined as 'An extensive unconscious life plan' (Berne, 1961) and is said to have developed in early childhood under parental influence. When presented with the idea that their current predicaments may have their origins in decisions made in early childhood in the face of limited options, high anxiety and very little real power, clients may begin to accept that their historical self (one of the ego-states located in the Archeopsyche) did the very best it could. They may then see that change is not only possible but also life-enhancing because it is being made from a more resourced state, and will increase options and choices. There is no shame in this – only celebration of survival and ingenuity.

There may be grief over the acknowledgement of a reduced awareness through life and the loss of a life plan that at least made sense of the world, and when translated into games made people predictable and situations familiar. At the same time, this way of explaining existential decisions early on in life normalizes rather than pathologizes the situation.

In one of the schools in transactional analysis, called the redecision school, it is acknowledged that the script cannot be changed purely by updating the Adult and confronting contaminated thinking (the equivalent, in part, of irrational self statements in rational emotive therapy) because the script decision was originally made by the Child. Because of this we need to regress to the age and point at which the decision was made in order to reconnect with the energy together with the current resourcefulness to redecide from this point onwards. This requires a complex set of relationship demands on the therapist who, working alongside the Child and the Adult, needs to be aware of his/her relationship with both, and what is required by each.

Finally, as with anyone who has mastered a few approaches, and continues to learn others, I think that three main themes have emerged:

One is that nowadays I am completely in the relationship, whether it is one of negotiating the therapeutic alliance, or the I–thou, or the developmentally needed reparative relationship or the transferential relationship or the transpersonal or all or some at once. I am aware of being fully engaged, not thinking theory, but there.

Second, I am also aware that, at any given time, I can step outside and self-supervise as I have the frames and theories that can help me find sign-posts in the landscape over which I am travelling with my clients. I know that I am influenced by some of the great teachers I have had, over time, and will call on some of their modelling and ideas to help me to be fully present in the service of the client. I also know that the notions of enquiry, involvement and attunement (Erskine et al., 1999) go beyond empathy in its traditional sense, being tailor-made to meet the rhythm, the affect, the relational need, the development stage and the cognition of the person sharing their walk with me.

Third, I am more and more aware that:

- my role is to enable my clients to unblock energy, often fixated in trauma, either recent or in the past, cumulative or single incident based;
- resolution of trauma is *always* relationally based, because trauma is not solely based on the incident itself, but on the fracture in relationship at the time of the event. Interventions in such circumstances include meridian-based therapies that use acupuncture points or acupressure points related directly to the emotions locked at the point of trauma, together with empathic attunement to the individual still suffering from phenomenological reoccurrence of the original trauma. These techniques include thought field therapy and the emotional freedom technique;
- the choice of intervention and the length of the therapeutic relationship are largely based on the assessment of the degree of trauma, the onset, in the developmental stage of the client and its nature. These factors lead me to assess whether the person needs counselling-based interventions or psychotherapeutic intervention, the level of dislocation to the person and the length of time he or she has suffered;
- the location of the trauma is not always primarily in the Child ego state, but can more often be found in one of the introjects (Parent). This will of course have profound effects on the Child but cannot be resolved simply from that part of the personality;
- self-support and living from the integration of the psyche (Integrated Adult) releases energy to be fully in relationship with self others and the world, and thus to be in a position to follow one's bliss (Campbell, 1976).

I end, as I began, with a sense of the sublime spiritual nature of the encounter, and a sense of grace that often occurs in the real meeting. The other day, I was working with a person from Zimbabwe, and in beginning to work with the loss of so much, we decided to do it through a sand tray, with me being witness, to this lovely person weeping goodbyes, with dignity and in Ndebele.

Transactional analysis is a truly integrating psychotherapy, providing humanistic principles alongside the rigour of psychoanalytic thinking and cognitive behavioural and existential analysis. Transactional analysis is based on a number of precepts, not least the belief that humans beings are inherently good and aspire to becoming who they are truly meant to be. This is the notion of physis, and is at the root of all humanistic approaches, and to work in this subtle, respectful and compassionate way, where there is an exchange of gifts and energy, at its best, is truly a blessing.

Chapter 17
An application of body psychotherapy

JOCHEN LUDE

Introduction

I am going to focus on some selected basic principles of my work as a body psychotherapist that are humanistic. I work from a position that is generally client centred, with an openness towards the possibility of an authentic meeting of equals in the therapeutic relationship. I see clients for their potential, abilities and strengths, working towards love, consciousness, self-determination and self-actualization.

I have chosen to look at the power dynamics as they can manifest in the therapeutic relationship, and to write about the importance of being embodied as a psychotherapist and being clear about the intention in the contact. I illustrate how I work with breathing and how I integrate dreams in the context of working as a body psychotherapist.

Core belief

I believe that each person is unique in his emotional, mental, psychological and spiritual make-up. Just as no one has the same fingerprint, no one has the same imprint of his innate nature. Each person needs to be seen, met and treated from this vantage point. This means that I need to strive to find this particular uniqueness in each person and to be open and curious along the way. For me, psychotherapy is an exploration towards and a detection of the original seed of one's being, one's unique essence. This personal essence is like everyone's holy grail and needs to be protected against the messages coming from the outside. The degree of protection varies and for many it manifests as a massive defensive armour – character structure. I believe this personal essence bears all human potential, including the capacity for self-organization and healing.

It is this view that attracted me to body psychotherapy – the view 'that human beings operate from an inner core – the primary level – which is *per se* spontaneous, positive and life enhancing, having the capacity for self-regulation . . . The secondary level – the character armour – contains the distorted impulses . . .' (Eiden, 2002, p. 28).

Understanding power

One of the most significant influences in life is our experience of power. Children are exposed throughout their upbringing to the almighty power of parents, teachers and adults in general. In so many ways children are powerless in relation to grown-ups and the reality is that adults do really have *power over* children. Growing up within such a convention may constitute a basic belief saying: 'in order to have power, I have to have power *over* someone' and in reverse: 'I am powerless and weak as long as I can't change you. If I can change you, then I know I have power because I have *power over you.*' This belief underpins a power structure we find everywhere in society and its institutions. The only way to have and to maintain power over someone is to use force. This often evokes a counter force and can easily escalate endlessly. To use force is a misuse and often even an abuse of power.

I challenge this belief system whenever the opportunity arises by saying to the client 'you don't have the power, for example, to change your partner's behaviour, unless you use force, but if you want to change the situation you are in with your partner you have only the power to change yourself. You have to take the responsibility for change.' Of course, this is true also within the therapeutic relationship. As a psychotherapist I don't have the power to change my clients, although they might wish to hand over the power for a while to me. This will be part of the client's therapeutic process and I need to be aware of it and be sensitive in my responses, not to take advantage of this given position.

The following clinical example might illustrate the point I want to make: A young woman, at the time in her late twenties, came to see me in an emergency as she frequently suffered from severe panic attacks, which came without any warning signals. She lost her strength and the capacity to move. Several times she collapsed while she was out shopping. Her legs would not carry her any longer and she had to be brought home by an ambulance. At the time she was still living with her parents. For days she could not get herself out of bed. Although she was living just around the corner, she had to come by taxi to see me. She was very scared of the condition being incurable and that she might end up being confined to a wheelchair. In one session it was appropriate to say to her:

> I believe that your body wants to tell you something by responding in such
> a radical way to you. There must be something in your life you are doing at

present which is not right for you. Your body is stopping you by saying 'I am not going any further'. Any idea what it could be?

Gradually she realized that she could not say 'no' to her mother's constant demands. It happened one day when she came to see me that I had to use the second-floor therapy room while I saw her normally on the ground floor. She had to climb up the stairs and by the time she entered the therapy room she was out of breath and started to panic. She asked me to bring her a glass of water. I went downstairs to fetch a glass and thought it might be good to offer her also a few drops of Bach flower Rescue Remedy with the water. When I attempted to do this, she screamed violently at me. 'No, no, I don't want this, let me out of here.' Immediately I reassured her that she did not have to take the Rescue Remedy. She drank the water and when she calmed down after a short while, she felt guilty and was very apologetic towards me, having misbehaved so badly. I pointed out to her that she had just shown to me how capable she was of taking care of herself by saying clearly 'no' to something she did not want. I praised her behaviour. At this moment her whole body let go of its tension and tears built up in her eyes. This was a turning point and the ice had broken. When she left that day she walked home for the first time and did not need a taxi any longer after that session. Further to these spontaneous changes, the client had a felt sense of relaxing and expanding in her body as opposed to being in a state of hyper-arousal and tension. I could use her experience as a resource to help her with simple breathing techniques – for example, putting her hand on her belly and slowly inhaling and exhaling, counting each time up to six. It did not take long before she was able to move out of her parents house into her own home.

How can we understand this? A fixed belief pattern with its predicted negative outcome became utterly shaken and completely electrified by a positive response that the client had never experienced on an organismic level before. I see this as an example where change occurred as a 'spontaneous creation which arose by amplifying events in given channels of the client therapist interaction' (Mindell, 1989, p. 8).

Embodiment and intentionality

It is essential to me, as a body psychotherapist, to be in touch with my own body and be able to use it and its senses in relation to myself and my client. Being anchored in my own body I create space for myself, which allows space between me and the client. This spaciousness enables clients to get in touch with their own inner space.

It is extremely important for me to be clear in my intention while I am relating to a client. My intention, my inner attitude, has an impact on the client, and clients will have a response, different sensations and feelings that stem from the relationship they have had to their primary love object, the mothering person, and how they have internalized this joint venture by introjection, identification and ego identity (Kernberg, 1979, p. 33). They can sometimes be extremely subtle or even unconscious. In being aware of my intention and the response of the client, I gain an understanding of the client's make-up and I am able to explore it further.

I use a simple exercise in training courses to illustrate the power of an inner attitude. The client is asked to lie on the mattress with closed eyes, while the therapist sits beside the client. For five minutes the therapist will adopt an inner attitude of being quite anxious, concerned and over-protective and for another five minutes the therapist will sit beside the client being unfocused, wandering off, having his thoughts somewhere else. In both cases the therapist remains sitting on the same spot, not altering his body position at all. The client has been instructed before-hand that it is not important to guess the two attitudes but to be aware of what responses and sensations they have in their body while experiencing them. Clients report back having had various bodily sensations, such as wanting to stop breathing, getting cold shivers, wanting to turn away; or having warm tingling sensations throughout their body, feeling held and safe; or having different emotions like feeling abandonment, fear, despair, anger, emptiness, sadness; or love, desire, pleasure and joy. Clients and therapists alike are bewildered by the profound effect of a simple change of intention.

This touches on the effective use of somatic counter-transference as the energetic connection and non-verbal communication is a two-way process. As a body psychotherapist, my body becomes an essential tool in understanding how the client's process creates energetic, sensory and emotional changes within me, which give me insights into the client's feelings, defences and projections.

Knowing that the psychotherapist's inner attitude has such a strong effect, physical touch transmits the intention even more. Touching a client's body with respect and an intention of inviting 'what is' – 'what-ever wants to happen, let it happen' and having no investment in the outcome, creates a space in which client and therapist can enter a thera-peutic dialogue that can be entirely physical and non-verbal for quite a length of time. Dialogue, as defined by Socrates, is a conversation between two (or more) people in which the questioner guides the other person step-by-step towards realization.

Here is a typical example of a short dialogue between my hand and a client's belly (as if they were able to use words):

Hand: I can feel quite a strong knot there.
Belly: Yes, since you mention it I feel it too and it hurts.
Hand: Can you bear the pain?
Belly: Just about.
Hand: I want to apply a bit more pressure.
Belly: I am scared it will hurt even more.

Hand: It probably will and I will lessen the pressure after a very short time.
Belly: Well go ahead and give it a go.
Hand: How was this?
Belly: Not as strong as I thought.
Hand: Is it OK to play with that for a while and see what happens when I apply each time a bit more pressure?
Belly: Yes, I am quite curious myself.
Hand: I want to stay much longer on the knot and I am sure it will be quite painful, see if you can bear it.
Belly: I'll give it a try – I can hardly bear it – it's on the edge – what a relief, the knot dispersed the pain has gone – I feel warm all over.
Hand: Well done, now you can enjoy the comfort.

It is sometimes important to be immersed in the rich world of non-verbal relating. New and deeper dimensions can be missed when meeting the client only in the world of language. It is also crucial not to interpret or put words to the client's experience, and let the client's body tell the story.

Working with breathing

Breathing plays a fundamental part in my work as a body psychotherapist. Breathing is the bridge between the voluntary and involuntary system of the organism. We can voluntarily stop breathing or force our self to inhale and exhale very fast, and we involuntarily breathe when living our daily routine or when asleep.

A breathing cycle has four different stages: inspiration followed by a still point followed by expiration followed by a still point. In inspiration we take in what the world has to offer, at the still point we transform what we took in from the world so it becomes a part of our self, in expiration we give to the world what we have to offer, at the still point we remain connected to our self.

The breathing rhythm resembles the rhythm of the sea. Inspiration is the building up of the wave with its peak at the still point. Expiration is the falling of the wave with its bottom at the still point. Each inspiration is like being born. People with an overemphasis on the inspiratory tendency are afraid of letting go, of dying. They need to be supported for more release. Expiration is like letting go. People with a similarly overemphasized expiratory tendency are afraid of growing up, to be born. They need to be supported for more containment. The polarity of release and containment in the breathing represents the polarity of holding-in or letting-go of feelings.

People who stay in the head have a pattern of resistance against their out-breath. They might present a schizoid tendency. They are helped to breathe out by encouraging an uncontrolled flow of movement. People who lose their heads and are overwhelmed by their feelings have a pattern of restricting their in-breath. They might present a hysterical tendency. They are helped by means of encouraging more containment.

The pulsation exercise that I describe below has all the potential to expose one's habitual breathing patterns. I also use this exercise for gathering diagnostic information about the underlying psychological defences.

The client kneels on the edge of a mattress with toes touching the floor, facing a pile of pillows. The therapist gives the following instructions:

> Be aware of your in-breath and out-breath and find your own rhythm. Take your time. When you feel you are in your rhythm imagine in your mind that your upper body moves slightly backwards with your in-breath and slightly forward with your out-breath. When you have a clear image in your mind only then let the image guide your body gradually into a physical rocking movement.

The aim of this exercise is to deepen the breathing capacity by increasing gradually the rocking movement and trying to keep the in and out breaths balanced. Continuing this movement, synchronized with breathing, mobilizes the energy flow throughout the body. Gradually the movements become more involuntarily and the body's defensive patterns are emerging, often accompanied by intense feelings as the underlying imprinted template is surfacing. The therapist's skilful physical intervention at this moment can guide and direct the charged energy flow through a holding pattern, setting free even more energy.

When using this exercise in a training group, a student got in touch with her long-held deep fear. By not giving up and staying with it, being supported by the regular pulsational movement, she reached the point when she would habitually give in and collapse, but this time could tap into deeper energy resources within herself, enabling her to let out a very deep-rooted life-giving scream. The sound was awesome for all members in the group and sent shivers down our spines. The release was followed by a tremendous energy surge throughout her body, culminating in an immense sense of joy and feeling reborn. The student reported later: 'I just can't believe what has happened, I recognize now that my fear always had controlled me and now I know I can control my fear.'

Integrating dreams

I am regularly working with groups of psychotherapists who want to add a bodily dimension to their existing way of working and who have committed themselves to ongoing body work. They agree to work on themselves either with me in front of the group or with each other within the group. In doing so, they experience body work first hand. The right brain receives information from the autonomic nervous system (ANS) about the state of the body. We take plenty of time in sharing the body sensations and feelings, as well as contributing theoretical and practical knowledge they have from their previous training, while I comment on methods and techniques that I have applied and substantiate them with theory and concepts of body psychotherapy. Talking and thinking through verbal language activates the left brain – so that putting into words what is felt/perceived in the body integrates the two hemispheres. The process of learning becomes more wholesome and profound by having added the organic component, as all aspects must be engaged in order for change to be deep, meaningful and long lasting.

It is essential for participants to feel safe and contained in the group and with me. This is often established relatively swiftly and the group gradually progresses into a 'body' in its own right, thus becoming a container for the individual working in the group. Every day we start with an opening round and participants are encouraged to share their dreams. I experience again and again that working directly with the body stimulates the dream factory and as the body releases blocked energies, dreams often occur more intensely. In sharing the dream images and motifs, the client gains more consciousness and the process of digestion and integration can unfold.

Here is an example. A male group member had done an intense piece of therapeutic body work the day before he had the dream. In his session he went through an extreme state of fear, his body being curled up in a frozen position and gradually being able to move out of it, culminating in an outburst of total rage, when his body expanded, being hot and sweaty and almost out of control. He shared the following dream the next morning. He was at a party in a room with a fireplace. The fire itself was burning not in but outside the fireplace and was in the process of dying out. He tried to balance the fire very carefully towards the fireplace with a brush and a poker, feeling afraid that the brush would catch fire. He had to juggle the fire around all these people and was afraid that they would all leave the party. There was one man in particular standing out and he knew that if this man left the party everyone else would leave too.

We looked at his dream by drawing attention to the energetic composition of his body as he experienced it and as I perceived it in his session. We came to the following understanding of his dream: the fire – his own fire, his compassion and love was not in the place – the fireplace – where it actually belongs in order to get adequately nourished to burn – to live – to its full potential and at the same time to be contained enough to be safe and not to be dangerous to himself and/or others. The brush and the poker represent his feminine and masculine energy, but also women and men in his life. When he is in touch with his fire, he is afraid to cause pain to others, in particular to women. He is in a double bind. On the one hand, his fire will die if not handled and he will end up in a frozen position. On the other hand, he fears the fire growing out of control and becoming destructive. In both ways, people will leave him. The client identified the 'one man who stood out' as his father, who was a powerful and dominating person and a constant threat to him, to 'his fire'. As a child, he was not supported to own his fire, he had to keep it out of its place, he had to repress it. Only now and then, he got in touch with it and he became overwhelmed with fear, not able to find a balance. I became the container first for his fear and then for his rage in the body work we did before. Having experienced this impact of direct physical containment, he developed a need and desire for containment.

Conclusion

I have explored with selected examples how my work as a body psychotherapist represents a humanistic and holistic approach to psychotherapy. As a humanistic psychotherapist, I have a holistic view of the human being and address how body and mind are intrinsically related. Most of us need help in contacting and learning to trust the knowledge of our body. I see my role as body psychotherapist as facilitating a process in discovering the innate wisdom of the body and its potential for well-being, creativity and choice. Psychotherapy often focuses more on verbal and mental processes and communication, whereas body psychotherapy brings an awareness to the subtle body processes, sensations and feelings, present, but sometimes hidden in the language of the body.

For further reading see Boadella (1987), Dychtwaid (1986), Grand and Johnson (1998), Johnson (1994), Keleman, (1979), Kepner (1987), Kurtz (1990), Lowen (1958, 1975), Rosenberg (1985), Staunton (2002).

Chapter 18
A gestalt psychotherapy in process

JUDY GRAHAM

In this chapter I shall demonstrate how I work by using a case example over a six-month period. My hope is that I can describe the lively and bright contact that surrounds my work, with the subsequent change that develops in the relationship between client and therapist as a result of how I am working informed by gestalt theory, philosophy, and therapeutic interventions. The work highlights the gestalt principles of phenomenology, awareness, holism, dialogic relationship, and experiment/experiential enquiry. I have an underlying working assumption that the client is the expert on herself. I use my own process when it supports the therapy.

Background

J (age 45) came requesting help 'to feel less tense, make changes at work and to form relationships'. Her mood is low and she doesn't find much meaning in life. She senses that there is something that hadn't been resolved in her previous therapy and wants to do short-term therapy with me. She has a good job as a special needs teacher in an inner city school and is fluent in several languages. English is her mother tongue. She lives alone, has some friends, and no significant relationship. In her leisure time, she tends towards solitary pursuits.

J is the eldest child with two younger brothers. Her mother, who died six years ago, was severely depressed for most of J's childhood and was prone to periodic outbursts of shouting. Father was an old-fashioned patriarch imposing a strict regime on his family, often espousing sexist, racist and homophobic attitudes. The father, now elderly, is living at home although in and out of hospital. J visits him every other weekend and categorically refuses to succumb to the tacit pressure that she move in like a 'good daughter and care for your father'.

We agree an initial contract of 20 sessions.

Phenomenological approach

In the second session, I begin by noticing how she makes sense of the world. Applying a phenomenological method of enquiry when I sit with J, I notice how she uses her contact functions (sight, speech, hearing, touch, movement). I also notice my responses. She speaks in a quiet, monotone voice. I must listen carefully to hear what she is saying. She asks me to repeat myself when I say something complimentary such as 'your new haircut looks nice'. She often looks down when speaking and then makes eye contact halfway through the sentence. Her breathing is shallow.

> The phenomenological approach means trying to stay as close to the client's experience as possible, to stay in the here-and-now moment rather than *interpreting* the client's behaviour, to help him explore and become aware of how he makes sense of the world. In other words it helps the client know 'who he is and how he is'. (Joyce and Sills, 2001, p.16)

Now I become aware of how I worked in my psychotherapy on my monotone voice. I notice an impulse in myself to teach her how to 'find her voice', to help her feel safe enough with me to show me all of who she is. I feel affection for her. I decide to bracket off most of what I am experiencing and open myself to wherever J wants to go. My decision to 'bracket off' is to avoid contamination – the possibility of guiding her to express herself the way I might want her to. There does not seem to be any constructive use for my experiences at this moment. I return to my belief that she knows what she needs to do to become whole/more herself. I am now more available to enable her to discover what and how that is.

> Bracketing, however, is not about attempting to be *free* from preconceptions, attitudes or reactions. It is an attempt to keep us close to the newness of the here-and-now moment and avoid the danger of making hasty or premature judgements about the meaning of each client's unique experience. (Joyce and Sills, 2001, p. 17)

She takes little space in the room, always sitting in the same seat and moving sparingly unless invited to do otherwise. I'm aware of her vulnerability. I feel protective then cautious about touching her. An interest emerges in the polarity to the vulnerability – her toughness. What did she 'toughen herself up' for? How has she adjusted to the legacy of her childhood? What are the fixed patterns (gestalts) she uses to make contact? *Gestalt is a word of German origin that means whole or configuration.* What creative adjustments has she made? *Creative adjustment is a modification to find the best ways of meeting needs.*

Dialogic relationship

The philosopher Martin Buber (1970) wrote about an 'I–thou' attitude where one person meets another without any preconceptions but with total openness. It is this attitude of inclusion that I am using in the following extract from session eight.

At the end of the second month of weekly meetings, J enters and sits on the same side of the sofa where she has chosen to sit since we began.

J: [Speaking softly, looking down at the floor.] I went to the hospital yesterday
Me: What for?
J: My regular check-up. I have an ulcer on my tongue
Me: That must be uncomfortable
J: I have lichen planus, it is an autoimmune condition. It has been all over my mouth and limbs but is now only on my tongue.
Me: Does it hurt? Are you in pain?
J: Sometimes when I eat oranges or if I get too stressed
Me: Are you in pain now?
J: [Looking at me directly.] It's better than before.
Me: Is it hard to tell me that you are hurting?
J: I don't believe people will listen.
Me: I'm listening.
J: Yes, it hurts when I swallow. They want to do another biopsy. This can become cancerous.
Me: How do you feel about that?
J: It's scaring.
Me: I'm glad you told me this. I hope I can help.
J: It helps to tell you.

Staying with her present experience in the 'here and now', we made contact when she said 'I don't believe people will listen'. She noticed that I was listening and that I believed her. I felt then that she began to trust me.

Holism

As a gestalt psychotherapist, I work holistically with the mind–body connection and am fascinated by the physical manifestations of psychological issues. I see the body as a rich source of information about who we are. All too often in our analytic culture we disconnect our minds from our bodies. I help clients reconnect to/with their bodies in order to enable a more complete and fuller experience of themselves.

With J, I'm struck by the 'matter of fact', unemotional way she told me about her medical condition. I am aware of her reluctance to share her pain and her surprise at my interest in her pain. I wonder what she may be doing to herself. How has she learned to turn her action inwards? What would she like to do to the environment/others that she is doing to herself?

Gestalt theory identifies this turning in on/injuring oneself behaviour as *retroflection,* an adaptation/resistance to contact. *This mechanism is the one employed by people who do to themselves what they would like to do to other people or objects.*

I am interested in the location of the ulcer – an angry sore in her mouth, on her tongue. What is she not saying? To whom can she not speak? What is she holding back/holding in? I'm reminded of my own awareness work on how I made myself sick by holding back angry feelings. Having done similar work on myself I feel safe enough to allow J to do whatever she needs to do. I believe that J knows what she needs to do to help herself. I'm energized to create a safe, supportive environment for her to discover the disowned parts of herself.

To help me understand about autoimmune diseases, I consulted Dr Christiane Northrup's *Women Bodies, Women's Wisdom* (1998). In the chapter 'Beliefs are physical' she says:

> If we don't work through our emotional distress, we set ourselves up for physical distress because of the biochemical effect that suppressed emotions have on our immune and endocrine systems. For example, an auto immune disease means that the immune system attacks the body . . . it is getting a destructive message from somewhere deep in the body . . . it is not the *stress itself* that creates immune system problems. It is rather the *perception* that stress is inescapable – that there is nothing a person can do to prevent it – that is associated with immune system suppression. (Northrup, 1998, pp. 34–6)

Giles Delisle (1999, p. 153), a Canadian gestaltist, has also made a valuable contribution to working with mind–body connections. He translates the DSM-IV into gestalt terminology.

I guess that, as a child, it was dangerous to express herself, so she learned to hide. She shows some of the characteristics of an avoidant personality or (in gestalt terms) her process for organizing her field of experience is by expecting to be rejected/ridiculed, she acts as if it were already the case and rejects herself.

Experiment

Six weeks later J begins the session with the report that the biopsy is all clear. She say she feels relieved. I tell her that I have been researching autoimmune conditions and ask:

Me: What is an autoimmune condition?
J: You turn in on yourself
Me: Do you remember when the condition started?
J: When I was on holiday I became aware of feeling socially accepted by other teachers from my country. I was thrilled. One of my dreams come true. When I noticed my social acceptance, my tooth broke.

Me: What sense do you make of this?

J: I hear; 'DON'T GET A BIG HEAD. THEY DON'T REALLY LIKE YOU. IT WON'T LAST.'

Me: Who said that to you?

J: My mother . . . she never said anything nice to me . . . she only said things like: 'girls listen, know our place'.

Me: What do you feel about that now?

J: I have something to say about that.

Together we set up an experiment with the imaginary mother in the empty chair opposite J. *In the 'empty chair' the client places any character of her life with whom she has an unfinished situation.*

J begins immediately in an elevated voice.

J: Mother, I am speaking out! in other languages and in other countries. I learned to express myself freely when I left this country. Remember when you needed a German translation and you overlooked me (the ONE who had a qualification in German), and asked my brother? Asked my brother? [J stops speaking to mother and looks at me.]

Me: How are you now?

J: That felt good to do that.

Me: Are you aware that you are *speaking out* now in English?

J: I'm ambivalent in English . . . feel confused.

Me: Confused speaking in your MOTHER TONGUE?

J: It's hard to find my voice in English. Somehow it feels like I'm doing something wrong.

Me: You have a conflict raging on your tongue.

J: That's for sure.

As the session comes to a close we discuss the connection between speaking out and belonging:

J: I believe that if I express myself, something bad will happen

Me: *You have negative thoughts about yourself (projection).*

In the projection the person ascribes to others the attributes she rejects about herself.

J: I feel more alive in foreign countries, speaking foreign languages.

Me: [Listening and believing in her value in the world.] You say interesting things. I am interested in what you say. I appreciate how creative you were to discover yourself by leaving the country. And I refuse to collude with your negative self-image. I invite you to ask for feedback from me and others. Find out if your projections are real or imagined. What is past and what is present.

It may not seem like a challenge because my words were soft and caring. However, because J has a belief that no one cares, my caring and my honesty indeed challenges her negative thinking. I told her I want something good to happen for her.

In a dialogic therapy, the therapist shows his caring by his honesty more than by his constant softness. He not only allows the patient to be who he is, he allows himself to be who he is in response. (Yontef, 1993, p. 222)

J becomes tearful:

Me: What's happening?
J: You are saying something nice to me.
Me: Something good can happen when you express yourself.
J: Yes, it can.

I begin the next session by saying that I was reflecting on last week, wondering about J's ambivalence when speaking in English. I sense that she feels ashamed to express herself and think she might have a fixed belief (gestalt) that she cannot/must not speak out in her home country. I wonder if it is safer to be quiet?

I guess that this belief may have a connection to the ulcer in her mouth. I ask her what she thinks. She says that she believes there is a connection but feels confused about everything.

We continue to co-create a diagnosis. She is becoming interested in her process.

I invite her to brainstorm the words: MOTHER TONGUE, which emerged with great energy in the last session. She is interested and starts off with 'tongue-tied, mouthing-off, keep your mouth shut, hold your tongue, festering, tongue-twister'.

Later in the week, I continue to brainstorm MOTHER TONGUE with a colleague in peer supervision. We threw out ideas:

• Biting her tongue was being confluent with father's wishes that she be silent.
• The mouth is a container (like mother) holding something in and guarding something.
• Her tongue wasn't used with the people with whom she had original emotional bonds – they either destroyed her or 'let her rot' (neglected her). Her tongue is rotting away, eating itself up, destroying itself.
• She is fluent in several tongues. It became clearer that the work is about finding the self-support to undo the retroflection.

Initial contract ends

At the end of 20 sessions, J wants to carry on. She feels that she is benefiting from the sessions. I agree and recognize her commitment to growing herself. I acknowledge her courage.

J came into the next session looking worried and speaks about how difficult her father is being about allowing home visitors to help him do things in the house. She is trying to work with Age Concern to install home care services to enable him to live independently. He is being stubborn, unappreciative, and ordering people to do things the way he wants. I encourage her to stay with the conflicting feelings and see what emerges.

J: He makes me so angry.
Me: Tell me more.
J: He treats me like I wasn't there.
Me: What does that feel like?
J: Humiliating. It reminds me of the past when I would speak out and he would accuse me of 'showing off'. I only wanted to be recognized for my achievement.
Me: What was that like for you?
J: Everything had to be his way.
Me: Where was your mother when this was going on?
J: Oh, she was afraid of him and did everything he said.
Me: So, she didn't defend you.
J: I remember being frightened in the night and wanted to go in her bed. She refused me.
Me: You must have felt very alone.
J: Very . . . you know, noone wanted to hear what I had to say. I wasn't allowed to speak out . . . but that wasn't all. Feelings weren't allowed either.
Me: Sounds like there were a lot of rules in the house.
J: Father would disown me if I expressed emotion. I'm afraid of losing it . . . falling apart if I 'don't brace up'.
Me: That must have been extremely hard for you.
J: There weren't any affectionate comments or names like 'mommy or daddy'.

Experiment

J becomes aware of the connection to the problems she has in showing love to others. I remind her how easily she expresses affection to her students, how she knows what they need to hear, how to encourage them and acknowledge their achievements. Together we create an experiment with J as the teacher in school delivering a lesson on LOVE AND WAYS TO SHOW AFFECTION. She puts her father in the class as a student.

This quotation from Polster and Polster (1973, pp. 234–84) shows how in gestalt we work to 'be in the present' experience rather than talking 'about' it:

Gestalt experiments are always co-creations in which the therapist helps to articulate goals and actively participates in the new organisation. Compared to most other approaches, we are more transparent, disclosing and involved. The experiment in Gestalt therapy is an attempt to counter the aboutist deadlock by bringing the individual's action system right into the room. Through experiment the individual is mobilized to confront the emergencies of his life by playing out his aborted feelings and actions in relative safety . . . What it provides is a diverse body of techniques which help make therapy a live, current experience rather than one where someone may excessively talk *about* his life.

The importance of being in the present is emphasized by Perls, Hefferline and Goodman:

> As the experiment of therapy proceeds, the patient dares more and more to be himself. He voices the statement that elsewhere he could only think, and thinks the thought that elsewhere he could not acknowledge even to himself. The patient is taught to *experience himself*. Experience is the actual living through an event or events. (Perls, Hefferline and Goodman, 1951, pp. 14–16)

This was an opportunity for J to confront the *introjected* message (no one cares what I have to say). *An introject is a part of the environment/other which is perceived as part of the self.*

J delivers a wonderful speech and becomes emotional, tearful – sadness at what she hadn't had as a child. (This is how she knows what others need.) She tells her father what a good teacher she is and how she knows about showing affection to her students. She calls him 'daddy'. J deconstructed the introject and experienced that someone does care what she has to say.

> To eliminate introjects from your personality the problem is to become aware of what is not truly yours, and above all to develop the ability to bite off and chew experience so as to extract its healthy nourishment. (Perls, Hefferline and Goodman, 1951, p. 435)

After the experiment, we discuss that she became aware of how humiliated she had been by her father when he accused her of 'showing off'. She hadn't realized fully that the taboo on not speaking became extended to no expression of feelings. We talk about father's military style, his rules in the house and what it was like for a young girl to live there. I keep reenforcing what a difficult environment she grew up in.

J, for the first time, sees that her childhood <u>had</u> been difficult. She also begins to see how much energy she has invested in defending her parents over the years. I help her begin to get in touch with her shame and make the connection with her fear of criticism. Her face looks soft.

Awareness

Next week, J begins the session energetically,

J: I'm saying more of what comes into my head. I'm more spontaneous.
Me: What are you saying, who are you saying more to?
J: My colleagues.
Me: Do you want to tell me?

J:	Actually, it's more what I didn't say when someone said something about me.
Me:	What didn't you say?
J:	I didn't say 'thank you'. My observation report was positive but my achievements don't fill me up. I have no sense of completeness. [She makes a dismissive, brushing away movement with her hand.]
Me:	Do you see what your hand is doing? Can you do it again, more . . .
J:	It's . . .
Me:	Batting away?
J:	Compliments.
Me:	What compliments?
J:	Yes, there is always something more expected of me – by me.
Me:	Can I give some homework to this teacher sitting here with me?
J:	Of course.
Me:	Notice what happens when you take in – fill yourself up with valid-ation from the observer of your work. Read the report fully and see how you are then.

The following week

J starts the session talking about how she found the homework helpful (reading the report from the observer). She noticed her pattern of min-imizing positive comments paid to her. She even went so far as to act as if they weren't happening. She brought a succession of three dreams that she had consecutively the previous night. I invited her to tell the dreams as if they were happening in the present – dream them again now. They had a common theme: something good is happening, then a disaster occurs. I present the work on one dream now:

J:	I'm alone on holiday and meet some nice people in a café. At last I'm socializing, feeling good, then we go on a walk and I'm walking behind the others. They go on, leaving me on a crumbling, narrow bridge. It is a steep drop. I have vertigo and am afraid of falling off. [She stops and looks at me.]
Me:	What are you experiencing now?
J:	I'm feeling unwell now . . .
Me:	You don't feel well now, here in this country? [I am thinking about the previous reference to a taboo associated with her home country.]
J:	When I feel good . . . something kills it off?
Me:	What kills it off?
J:	Other people are dangerous.
Me:	What other people?
J:	All people
Me:	Do you really believe that about all people?
J:	I believe they won't like me.
Me:	So you make something happen that destroys the chance of finding out?
J:	Like batting away something positive?

Me: Exactly; what else could you do?
J: Wait and find out what happens.

J is breaking down the introject ('no one likes me'). She is beginning to see that she is doing something to herself based on old messages. She is beginning to question whether those messages are redundant. She is taking responsibility for noticing what she needs and exploring new ways of getting her needs met. She has a choice to maintain the old patterns or find something new.

Next session

J has had a hospital visit. The doctors want to do another biopsy because the ulcer has remained inflamed since Christmas. (Christmas had been a difficult time with many issues being restimulated.)

In the session, J got in touch with her fear of being trapped in the illness; being trapped in the vicinity of the hospital; being trapped in this country. She told me about her dislike of being dependent. I think of Dr Northrup's (1988) description of autoimmune conditions: 'it is the *perception* that the situation is inescapable'.

Then she recounted another dream:

J: I'm in a session with you. Various people are coming in and doing repairs in the room. You ask me 'I hope you don't mind?' and I answer 'no, of course not'. Then I say to myself 'what are you saying that for when you don't mean it?'
Me: How does this relate to us NOW? What is unsaid between us now?
J: I do remember feeling slightly angry with you . . . remember that session when I was ill? I had lost my voice? I had a sore throat . . . and . . .
Me: Oh yes, I kept asking you how you were feeling? We did the session anyway. Did I miss something?
J: You were writing notes.
Me: What about that?
J: I don't like that . . . it makes me feel like an object.
Me: Like something else is more important than you? What did you want from me?
J: Why were you writing?
Me: The book chapter, remember?
J: I wanted to be comforted. I needed mothering that night.
Me: I missed that.
J: When you asked if I was OK, I said I was fine to go ahead with the session.
Me: So you wanted me to just know what you needed, even if you told me something else?
J: It's hard to ask for what I need.
Me: I understand that and you are saying it now.

It was important that J was able to express her anger with me and discover that I didn't reject her . . . Something different happened. We became closer.

Weeks later

Some weeks later, J came into the session reporting an argument she had had with a colleague. She said that when she expresses herself she feels 'nasty and bad' and fears retaliation. She also noticed that she likes herself when she is the 'snappy J' who is quick witted with ideas and opinions. As we explore her experience together, J is becoming more aware of how she puts herself down by calling her behaviour 'childish' and seeing attention-seeking as only something bad, antisocial. She begins to discover the value of being noticed. She can now allow herself to be childlike, choosing when to grow herself up and challenge others. What she expects due to past experience does not always happen in the present.

J is changing by becoming who she is. Gestaltists name this process 'the paradoxical theory of change'.

Change occurs when one becomes what he is, not when he tries to become what he is not. Experience has shown that when the patient identifies with the alienated fragments, integration does occur. Thus, by being what one is – fully – one can become something else (Beisser, 1970, pp. 77–8).

A week later

J: I let it get to me.
Me: What?
J: I was so angry with a colleague
Me: And?
J: I couldn't stop myself saying something to her.
Me: Good, you let what is important to you mean something!
J: Yeah, I usually push it down and keep quiet.
Me: I'm enjoying your assertiveness. You are being more yourself. You are letting *you get to you.* 'Letting it get to me' was something to be avoided in the past. It meant that you were bothered or affected by something – being bothered was taboo. [I use her words to help her reframe the meaning of this behaviour.]

Conclusion

In the safety of the therapeutic relationship, J was able to experiment with new behaviour and thus discover how she was holding on to the past. She became aware of how this behaviour was redundant and not meeting her current needs. She then began the work to letting go of that pattern of being in the world and discovering how she wants to be now. With awareness comes choice. She grew in her appreciation of listening to her body. She now sees that her rebellion against her mother tongue was a creative adjustment in the past and she now needs to speak out in English.

I feel privileged to be accompanying J in the discovery of who she is becoming. Our work reminded me of how I too can lose my voice. As a result, I rediscovered my love of singing.

Chapter 19
Why I am a humanistic practitioner (and a Winnicottian with a Buddhist meditation practice)

DAVID JONES

First experience of psychotherapy

For personal reasons, I underwent psychoanalysis during the 1960s, first of all with a trainee and then with an experienced member of the British Psychoanalytic Society. In those days psychiatrists offered behaviour therapy. I did not like the sound of it because of its impersonal, mechanical nature. RD Laing and his colleagues wrote books criticising psychiatry, which I enjoyed reading, but as I did not feel drawn to their anti-society rhetoric I did not seek help from them, although many of my friends did. Freudian and Jungian therapy was the only alternative, but that was not widely available, being limited almost exclusively to Harley Street in central London and Belsize Park, a small area of north London.

I lay on a couch for 50 minutes five days a week and said the first thing that came into my mind, including the details of what had happened since the previous session, memories of childhood, trouble with girlfriends and dreams, when I remembered them. My analyst sat out of sight. He was strongly influenced by Winnicott, whom he spoke of in hushed tones. I read Winnicott's work and liked its insights, especially about childhood. I heard him lecture at the London School of Economics and could see why so many people liked him as a person. I especially like his ideas about play as preparation for the adult world, about the necessity for a secure holding environment from which a child explores its world (repeated in the therapy setting), about transitional objects, and so on. I was impressed by the fact that he began to explore touch with patients to facilitate regression to perinatal states of experience. Margaret Little describes the value of this in an excellent book (Little, 1987), which is largely ignored by analysts for whom touch is still anathema (Jones, 1994).

When I was pronounced analysed, I continued to feel disturbed and often seemed to disturb other people. I was left with the impression that the analysis benefited my therapist. He felt more comfortable with me once he could fit me into his frame. The only parts of the therapy that touched me were when there was some personal contact. This came about when I realized he was homosexual, when he laughed and when he accepted a bottle of whisky from me in the last session with the words 'but how did you know I was a whisky man?'.

Something was missing from my experience of psychotherapy. I did not know it at the time but analysts were coming to the same conclusion (Torronto, 2002; Kahn, 1991 – Chapter 5 has an excellent account of the leading American analyst, Kohut's views). My therapist was not available to me as a person. This created a relationship that was so meagre that therapeutic change was barely possible. The transaction with him was also limited to conversation. I found it hard to listen to him, being close to sleep on the couch. So much of what he said went in one ear and out of the other. Later on I realized that, in addition to looking at the experience of transference and counter-transference in the therapy room, psychotherapy also needs experiential exercises so that embodiment can also be integrated with conscious thought and feelings. I learned that a good way of doing this is to facilitate experiential exercises (see below) with clients having control over what they do and how far they go with it. In doing this we should not deny the importance of the counter-transferential revolution in psychoanalysis. Feeding back to clients what I experience them as trying, unconsciously, to pull out of me is very important. But trying to do that is to be absent from any relationship with my client, as if I am sitting behind a one-way mirror like a scientist looking at a specimen. I found this bizarre when I experienced it. Besides, the humanistic exercise of getting clients to recapitulate what they have heard tells therapists how effectively they are communicating.

As soon as my analysis was over I sought the missing ingredient in the humanistic approach to therapy or the development of human potential, as it was often called. The encounter movement was in full swing in the 1970s and early 1980s and I entered fully into it, discovering the humanistic legend at first hand and culminating in a two-year training with the Institute for the Development of Human Potential (IDHP), an organization that, unfortunately, died once the encounter movement, with all its excesses, came to an end. Reading the first editions of John Rowan's books (Rowan, 1976, 1983; Reason and Rowan, 1981) was an eye opener to me for their lively and sensible views in a difficult area. Again, I did not know it at the time, but I was moving with the times, following the history of the development of modern psychotherapy.

I became a practitioner running gestalt groups and working with individuals. Later I trained in core process psychotherapy at the Karuna Institute, a psychospiritual approach based on the Buddhist model of the mind. The mindfulness that this develops is akin to the counter-transferential revolution in analysis. The therapist's awareness of his own active process in the therapy room combines with the client's and is used for the benefit of the client. In order to develop and maintain my equanimity, compassion for others, loving kindness and sympathetic joy for others' achievements, I have a daily meditation practice that is Buddhist based with some Hindu influence. I also go on residential meditation retreats. This has improved my relationship with my own experience. The main effect visible to other people is that it keeps me calm.

I also came to the conclusion that all approaches to therapy have short-comings as well as strengths. The psychospiritual approach tends to disapprove of people who like male qualities, has difficulty with anger and sexuality, preferring to witness feelings at the expense of learning to express them with competence.

In Britain, the great bulk of development in the psychoanalytic approach to the body is carried within the humanistic and integrative community by the post-Reichian people such as Staunton (2002), Totton (1998) and West (1994) and also by practitioners of gestalt, transactional analysis, and psychodrama, and some of the transpersonal approaches, all of which have roots in psychoanalysis. This puts the humanistic and inte-grative people, secretly, at the cutting edge of developments in psychoanalysis, a point that few people like to recognize (Torronto, 2002).

Other psychoanalytic work is important to me as well, but it usually comes into play only with particular clients. For example, Jung's para-doxical idea that a psychotic breakdown is protecting a client's sense of self from disintegrating and losing its unifying and integrating function (Searles, 1993) helped me with Arthur.

> Arthur had been in hospital for a year diagnosed and treated for drug induced psychosis. We developed the idea that he had reacted to his ex-perience of rejection and bereavement in early childhood by preserving his sense of himself through going crazy. We saw it as the price he paid for deal-ing with his fear of fragmenting into nothingness. This paradoxical way of looking at it seemed to help though it took several years before he ceased medication, got a menial but adequate job and began a professional train-ing. It gave me the confidence and a sense of direction in responding to his insatiable demands that he be seen and heard.

My current practice

For the past 20 years I have been in private practice in south London and, for five years, also had a practice in north-west Devon. People hear of me mainly by word of mouth, although the registers are relevant, and come to me with a great variety of difficulties. Loss, especially bereavement; depression; difficult relationships at work and at home; sexual and iden-tity problems; and pain associated with the biological clock are typical.

Whereas personality issues usually play a part in creating and main-taining these difficulties, the social and political milieu in which the person is embedded is always a source of contributory factors. Childhood and subsequent experience are, of course, important but I have learned that it is not always helpful in dealing overtly with these interlocking causal matrices. The healing process is a mystery and it is not always obvious what has led to personal growth and the reduction of suffering. Useful therapy involves some or all of the following that usually occur in no particular sequence: becoming aware of perceptions, especially projections; getting in touch with feelings and feeling them fully; choosing what to do as a response rather than a reaction; and noticing how things have changed as a result of action, especially the effect on other people.

I am careful with explanations or analysis of facts and causes because change can occur in so many different ways. Intellectual understanding of the client often happens after therapeutic change has occurred and may give satisfaction to me 'as therapist' as a device for making sense of a confused and confusing situation rather than bringing relief to my client, although it can do that too. New clients usually want to talk.

> Peter is a middle-aged man whose way of working had broken down. He was on medical sick leave and had recently ended yet another tempestuous relationship. He described his bleak childhood and his tumultuous adolescence presenting rich material for us to work with. Having done that in the first few weeks he began to fall asleep during sessions. He told me briefly what had happened since I last saw him and then fell asleep for anything between half an hour and forty minutes. I wrestled with practicalities like finding another time when he was less tired so that he could 'get his money's worth' and 'get something out of the sessions'. I wondered if he was fleeing from the prospect of engaging with the terrible feelings that lurked within him. He seemed happy to sleep during the sessions. He said it made him feel better. Eventually it dawned on me that this was the work. I think he was learning to trust me and trust was something he had not had much opportunity to develop in his life so far. Just being asleep in my presence made something shift. The underlying causes of this change are, however, obscure and in that sense a mystery.

Types of intervention and types of therapeutic relationship

Telling of their experience and difficulties and discussing some aspects with me is of course part of the 'mysterious' process of therapeutic change. But *analytic* explanation is only one of a number of useful interventions. Facilitating exercises that act as a *catalyst* to the client's inner processes; *catharsis* of feeling; a modicum of appropriate *self-disclosure* by me, are all equally potent psychotherapeutic interventions. Indeed, the very way I structure and, in a sense, *direct* interaction in my therapy room is also part of this potency. Dyed-in-the-wool person-centred therapists may deny it, but they are in fact structuring their therapy sessions and being directive just as much as any other therapist in the way they furnish their rooms and by insisting that the client determines what happens next. John Heron (1990) gives a comprehensive description of these six types of intervention. Superordinate is the importance of warm support felt by the client and offered by the therapist, not as a collusive arrangement but as a form of unconditional love.

The presence of the therapist is crucial. The therapist should come across with a warm concern for the client. Psychoanalysts recognize this, although traditionally they have taken the view that being visible to the client muddies the transference and makes analysis more difficult. Humanistic therapists allow clients to feel they are fully present in the relationship. This means being attentive and, although they should not argue their opinions and views and should not go on at length about themselves, they respond to their clients as fully present individuals. When addressed by the client, they reply. I always respond to a greeting and enquiry about my health briefly and accurately. If I am asked about myself, my holiday plans or family, I respond with a brief answer and when it feels appropriate suggest that my client says how my response affects them. I sometimes ask them why they are asking me, why they want to know the answer to their enquiry about me. Petrūska Clarkson has described the many ways in which clients relate to therapists. Her work influenced my development. (Clarkson, 1993, 1995).

Basic goodness

Humanistic practitioners have a positive view of all clients, seeing them as essentially valuable people. The fundamental humanistic belief is that everyone (including the therapist) possesses within them a natural healthy force toward regeneration.

This means that no matter what damaging experiences we have had, whatever damaging transgression or, to use the modern terms, abuse or atrocity has been visited upon us, we still have the potential to develop. It is possible to recognize and transcend states of shock, defensiveness and amnesia so that we develop towards a more healthy way of being in the world, towards realizing our full potential as good humans. The purpose of therapy is to facilitate this process.

> Melissa, a middle-aged woman, came to see me for bereavement counselling after her husband had died. After some 20 sessions, during which we focused mainly on her loss and regaining her liveliness, she began to expand on traumatic events to which she had previously alluded and which she could only partially remember. These had occurred when she was a girl in her country of origin. She described how police or soldiers (she was unsure which) had come to the house where she was staying with her

brother and taken them to a prison or barracks where she was made to watch whilst her brother was tortured and killed. She was sexually and sadistically abused. Hurt, and left in a 'cupboard' on her own in the dark she formed a plan to escape. Her escape took several hours to carry out and required adjustment to her plan as she went along. Luck was also on her side. There was a point as she was telling her story that I noticed my body go into shock, my mind into evasion. My inner dialogue started up: 'Do not retraumatise this woman.' 'Surely this can't be true.' Feelings of sorrow welled up in me. I realized I had stopped listening. I interrupted Melissa and said, briefly, that I was in shock, that I felt sorrow at what had happened to her. Instead of interrupting her process, as I feared it might, my intervention seemed to deepen the relationship between us and enabled her to continue exploring her experience over the coming months more slowly and reflectively. I applauded her determination and skill and said how glad I felt that she was alive. As months of weekly therapy were now rolling into years, Melissa explored a number of things, including her reaction to fragments of memory associated with certain sounds, smells and images. The shadowy image of a man began to emerge at which she was able eventually to direct pent up emotion. This image of a man seemed to stand for more than one actual soldier or policeman. She explored, using cushions, what she would like to do to 'him'. Amidst tears and laughter she used her commitment to Christianity to find a place in which she discovered she was doing to him what he had done to her and moved a long way towards forgiveness of him and forgiveness of herself.

The force leading to health is illustrated by the above: 'positivity' was hidden in the 'negative'. There is a consequence to this type of progress, though, which clients and therapists, who believe that issues can be resolved once and for all, find difficult to accept. As the client's suffering reduces, another set of painful issues can kick in and the client may come to suffer more, not less. This makes personal development in and out of therapy, and for both therapist and client, an endless roller coaster lasting all our lives.

Experiential exercises

Experiential exercises are important to the humanistic approach: a feature shared by NLP (neurolinguistic programming), Ericksonian hypnotherapy and cognitive behavioural therapy (CBT). Learning about one's self, discovering patterns, interrupting them, discovering how one perceives things, framing experience, getting in touch with feelings and reactions can be completed only experientially. This puts serious limits on classical psychodynamic therapies with their reliance on conversation and analysis of transference, for without experiential exercises this type of conversation is incomplete. It lacks ways of accessing pre-verbal material.

Therapy can help address suffering and disturbed behaviour by enabling people to transform the hurt, and the defences against hurt, caused by distress arising in childhood, and later on, which comes about due to invalidation and deprivation of what we need. Doing experiential exercises so that stuck emotions and feelings are explored and expressed, and in the end accepted as friends, lies at the heart of my approach. I do this in a client-centred way in that I encourage clients to take charge of deciding what, out of the exercises and foci for discussion that I offer them, they will do and how much they will focus on memories from child-hood and later.

Limitations

I respect individual choices regarding how life is to be fulfilled; lifestyle, religious and political beliefs and the expression of sexuality, so long as they do not invalidate, deprive or in other ways harm other people. I make clear, when necessary, that I can work with people only if they refrain from over-use of intoxicants (alcohol, cannabis mostly but also caf-feine). Where it is relevant, I tell clients I cannot work with them if they continue to threaten overtly suicidal behaviour. They must have a suffi-cient commitment to being alive. (I am no expert at working with people with serious eating disorders or serious addictions. I am willing to see them occasionally so long as they establish a working relationship with specialist agencies.)

Other important issues

Education of the affect as well as the intellect is important, leading to emotional competence, the ability to access feelings, feel them and express them in appropriate ways. This means catharsis in appropriate contexts, sitting on them or bottling them with awareness or witnessing them. Asking clients to put their hands on the part of their body where they most feel the feeling draws attention to the bodily base of feelings. But it goes further than that. Reich pointed out that defences are embodied.

Celebration of who we are, what we experience and what we have achieved is often debased. Instead of giving recognition to it all, basking in it, elaborating on it and putting it in the foreground, there is often a tendency to put it behind us and to move on to the next thing. Or, worse still, to have a party 'to celebrate' in which alcohol creates tipsy joviality, which can feel good but actually robs us of the possibility of celebration.

Lifelong disciplined growth. Psychotherapy can be about solving imme-diate problems and difficulties. But it soon becomes apparent that the process of doing this is endless. A better strategy is to see psychotherapy as part of personal growth, which continues to the day we die. We are continuously discovering more about ourselves.

Autonomy and co-operation, not competitiveness. So much of life is set in a competitive frame. From birth, babies are measured to see if they are thriving. The downside of this is that to be at the lower end in size or weight implies failure. Light babies are diagnosed as 'failure to thrive'. Learning in school is measured with the same consequences. Making cash, owning consumer goods, keeping up with the Joneses is given great emphasis. It is part of the humanistic canon that this is emphasized too much. In my work with clients I often suggest they experiment with getting their needs met in a co-operative way rather than a competitive one.

Guru-ization should be tolerated but moved away from. Training institutes and groups of practitioners tend to develop strong in-group identities, often idolizing their teachers, supervisors and role models around whom they form an adoring group. This is inevitable, but if it becomes chronic it inhibits the development of practitioners for it prevents them becoming their own gurus, which is an aim of therapy. It is also tiresome for outsiders to be met with such a laager-like impenetrable structure. Following respected guides as authorities is helpful; obeying them uncritically and bathing in their charisma is to join an authoritarian group that can develop into a cult. The human potential movement in Britain in the late 1970s fell collectively into this trap. A large proportion of the leading humanistic practitioners of the day joined the Rajneeshi movement and became Orange people. For various reasons, most, but not all of them, soon left. (For my account of this see Jones 1987.)

Therapeutic exuberance should be recognized and lovingly discouraged. Having a good experience in a workshop or therapy session is a marvellous thing and wanting others to have it too is very understandable, but clients have to find their own way and may not react the same way as you do. Therapists should have no expectations about how a client will respond to a particular exercise or intervention even if the therapist got a lot out of it. Still less should therapists believe that a client who has not been helped by a series of exercises or interventions has not completed the therapy, or not done it right. This is like saying the client is to blame for failure (a version of blaming the victim) whereas the reality is that therapy or therapist has not been right for the client at that point on the client's path to health. It may help clients to discover how they avoided, sabotaged even, the therapist's attempt to assist them, but this should be seen as the clients' way of defending themselves and not as their failure or due to something wrong with their approach to therapy.

Touch and bodywork. Although Winnicott began to incorporate touch in his work (Little, 1987) and a tradition of therapeutic touch is used by many bodyworkers in the UK (Staunton, 2002; Totton, 1998 and Jones, 1994), I have largely refrained from using it. Until now, I have been anxious about it, not trusting myself to be competent about the feelings it might arouse in me, especially sexual feelings and feelings of revulsion. I offer exercises involving body awareness but avoid touch. This is something I need to look at in my own continuing professional development.

I am aware that practitioners in this field have, like the humanistic people, developed their theories from Freud mainly through the work of Reich and his followers. Today's orthodox Freudians, who may call themselves psychoanalysts, are wont to say – as the proponent of a Private Member's Bill to regulate psychotherapists, Lord Alderdice did – that humanistic and bodywork therapists are not really psychotherapists. However, these are the approaches that are capable of producing the most profound personal change, rather than the adaptations to society's norms aimed at by Freudian analysts. These critics are also blind to the cutting-edge developments that are going on in the disciplines that make up the humanistic and integrative approaches to psychotherapy.

Chapter 20
A humanistic integrative approach to psychotherapy

Maria Gilbert

My approach to psychotherapy is underpinned and informed by a basic belief in the capacity to heal and change in all people, which enables them to free themselves from the unnecessary constraints of their past 'scripts' (Berne, 1972) in creating a new narrative for themselves in the safe environment of the therapy. This capacity to realize human potential, described as 'self-actualization' by Maslow (1970), had already been elaborated by Berne (1947/1957) in his concept of 'physis', which he defined as 'the force of Nature, which eternally strives to make things grow and to make growing things more perfect' (Berne, 1957, p. 68). Berne considers physis an inborn drive or capacity that exists in all people, naturally leading them to seek what is best for themselves within the constraints of a given situation.

Berne's concept of scripting stresses the influence of parents and the early environment as powerful shaping influences on the child's narrative about life and its possibilities. 'Scripts are artificial systems which limit spontaneous creative human aspirations' (Berne, 1972, p. 213); implicit in the use of the word 'artificial' is the belief in the possibility of regaining a spontaneous way of life. In the interests of survival, therefore, the child may be pushed to make certain self-limiting decisions that can have a powerful unconscious influence on her life course but there is always the presence of 'physis', which leads people in the direction of growth and change. This belief in the person's capacity to grow and self-regulate is also embedded in the gestalt therapy concept of 'creative adjustment' (Perls, Hefferline and Goodman, 1951/1994, p. 22), which supports an optimistic view of human potential, in maintaining that people's desires 'will spontaneously regulate themselves, and if they have been deranged, they will tend to right themselves' on condition that people are 'let to be' (Perls, Hefferline and Goodman, 1951/1994, p. 24). This belief in an inborn human capacity to search for change and growth given supportive conditions places my approach to psychotherapy firmly in the humanistic tradition. However, it is important to take into account the very real limitations in the lives of many people who are struggling with issues such as war and poverty, illness and social deprivation, where the drive for self-realization may be thwarted or suppressed by the bleakness of daily existence. A naive optimism in the face of economic, political and social realities can, I believe, be an insult to the everyday struggles that clients are facing.

What first attracted me to humanistic approaches to therapy is their emphasis on the crucial importance of respect for self and for the person of the other. Transactional analysis developed this into the concept of 'I'm OK with me – you're OK with me' (Stewart and Joines, 1987, p. 19) to show how this attitude of respect refers to a person's frame of reference with regard to others. I can hold this position of valuing others even when they feel 'not-OK' with themselves and so 'invite' them into an OK position in their lives. Of course, no one feels OK all of the time and the art of the challenge in therapy and in life is to learn to support ourselves in those times when we drop into feeling not-OK with ourselves! An ability to soothe ourselves is important for therapists and clients alike in times of stress.

Sometimes, as a therapist, I will need to hold this 'I'm OK–You're OK' position consistently over time in relation to a client before the client feels sufficiently supported to feel OK about himself. This can be a particular challenge when we are on the receiving end of a client's anger or disdain – for example, it may be a challenge to stay OK with yourself as a therapist when a client is saying 'this therapy is no good – I sometimes wonder what I am paying you for. I would be better off trying to solve this on my own!' To remain OK with myself and at the same time consider what truth there may be in the client's statements is at the heart of the matter here.

Espousing the value of the 'I'm OK – You're OK' position means that I strive to attain and maintain this attitude in relation to clients and deal openly with times when I may 'slip' from this. Contracting in a therapeutic context is a way in which respect for the other can be built into the therapeutic process. If I am open to sharing the process of agreeing goals with a client and being clear and open about the methods of the therapy I am using and get the client's agreement to these, then I can foster an open process with clients. Such transparency means that the therapeutic relationship is co-constructed by both of us as participants and that I as the therapist do not have a 'secret agenda' hidden from the client. This demonstrates a respect for the client's ability to know what is best for herself and to share equally in the therapeutic process. 'I want to emphasize my belief that a careful search with the patient for the change goal that most fully captures the person's struggle with pains and frustrations relative to the story of his or her life is a key part of the building of a strong therapeutic alliance' (Horvath and Greenberg, 1994, p. 19). I may also sometimes have a dearly held position about what strategies may help with certain problems and goals of the client's and may try to impress these on the client. For example, using two-chair work to explore the client's internal dialogue may well hold more appeal for me than for the client and rather than insisting or labelling this resistance I may need to call on my humility and respect for the client's view of what is helpful to her!

An additional emphasis in humanistic practice implicit in the belief in human potential is a belief in personal responsibility and in a person's capacity for choice and therefore change that underpins my practice. The assumption is that when the person is unhindered by demands and negative pressures, she will become aware of and choose what is best for her. However, a humanistic approach to psychotherapy need not exclude a respect for the power of unconscious processes, a feature of human experience that has sometimes been glanced over in humanistic therapies so that they may seem to be naively optimistic and underrate man's capacity for evil, whether this be driven by unconscious processes or whether it be the result of conscious choice. An over-optimistic trend within some humanistic practices has led critics to see humanism as a whole as perhaps overlooking the darker side of human nature. I have come to realize that an acceptance of the power of unconscious process for better or for worse does not negate the person's capacity for change and choice; it does, however, warn against a surface acceptance of visible phenomena and ask for a more thorough exploration of underlying dynamics, a position which is clearly shared by Berne in this definition of script: 'A script is an ongoing life plan formed in early childhood under parental pressure. It is the psychological force which propels the person toward his destiny, regardless of whether he fights it or says it is his own free will' (Berne, 1972, p. 32).

The meta-analysis of previous outcome research by Luborsky et al. (1975, quoted in Wampold 2001), which clearly confirmed the central importance of the therapeutic relationship as one of the main common factors in the process of change, has led to an increased research focus on the quality of the therapeutic alliance (Horvath and Greenberg, 1994; Wampold, 2001). Subsequent research, in particular the recent meta-analysis of outcome research since 1975 conducted by Wampold, has supported an acceptance of the power of the therapeutic relationship as the most important healing factor across different types of psychotherapy (Wampold, 2001). The provision of an effective healing relationship is what we all share despite differences in philosophy and technique! In keeping with these research findings, which stress the healing nature of the therapeutic relationship, I feel well supported in a relational approach to psychotherapy based on a humanistic philosophy that likewise stresses the central importance of the therapeutic relationship as the vehicle for change. The building up of a good and solid working alliance is the basis for any further work together. The working alliance is 'an attachment that exists to further the work of therapy and contains participants' role expectations regarding the work of therapy' (Gelso and Carter, 1994, p. 300).

The context in which the relationship develops will influence the expectations of both participants; for example seeing a therapist in a GP practice where sessions are limited will be vastly different from seeing a private practitioner where both participants can jointly negotiate the parameters of the relationship (such as length of therapy). Another factor that is being increasingly emphasized in the therapeutic literature is what each of the participants brings to the relationship in terms of background, culture, race, class, gender, age and the other myriad individual nuances and differences that distinguish us as unique. In this sense, every thera-peutic relationship is a unique co-creation between two individuals in a never-to-be-repeated constellation at a particular point in history. The contextual sensitivity of each therapeutic relationship means that I, as therapist, need to be particularly alert to the factors that may be influenc-ing each of the unique therapeutic relationships in my practice. A good question that I frequently ask of myself is: 'who may I be representing for this client at this point in time given who I am and how I am presenting myself?' (Transference operating in the here-and-now.) Equally relevant for me is the question: 'And who may the client be representing for me?' (Counter-transference operating in the here-and-now.).

From its inception, humanistic therapy has focused on the crucial importance of the 'real relationship' (Gelso and Carter, 1994, p. 303), which refers to the real meeting between two human beings, which for me remains a strong central focus in my work over my years of practice. The real sense of meeting between two people makes the possibility of genuine dialogue possible. The idea of healing through meeting is also central to a contemporary gestalt approach to psychotherapy (Hycner, 1993) which focuses on the co-creation of the relationship between ther-apist and client and believes that healing happens in the 'between'. A good working alliance forms the basis for such a meeting, which involves my willingness as a therapist to be fully present to the client as one human being to another in the here-and-now of the therapy process (Hycner, 1993). Presence is 'a recognition of the mysteriousness and interpenetration of our existence' (Hycner, 1993, p. 122); he later adds 'It's somewhat like riding the rapids of a river – you need to constantly flow with it, and respond moment by moment to the ongoing changes' (Hycner, 1993, p. 123). This ever-changing dynamic flow of the therapeu-tic relationship marks the quality of the real relationship in humanistic approaches to working with clients. Such an approach requires of me, as the therapist, a willingness to give of myself to the other without hiding behind theory or technique!

An interesting recent development in psychotherapy outcome research into the 'common factors' that contribute to change in the therapeutic process is the current focus on the client's self-healing capacities as per-haps the most important of the factors common to all psychotherapies as healing processes. This may seem self-evident to a humanistic practition-er who has held all along to the importance of the process of client self-actualization as central to change, but it is important to note that in most of the outcome research over the past five decades that has focused on the healing power of the therapeutic relationship the research empha-sis has been on the qualities supplied by the therapist rather than on what the client brings to the relationship. This 'therapist-as-hero' approach in research and writing (Hubble, Duncan and Miller, 1999, p. 94) even per-meated the research into client-centred therapy where the therapist provision of the 'core conditions' has tended to be emphasized as the essential components of the healing process. This almost exclusive focus on the therapist's activities and their importance to the change process suggests an exaggerated reverence for the therapist's contribution to the detriment of the client's. Hubble, Duncan and Miller rather wryly use an African proverb to underline this surprising tendency of therapists to pri-oritize their own importance in a profession that is geared to helping clients. 'Until lions have their historians, all tales of hunting will glorify the hunter' (Hubble, Duncan and Miller, 1999, p. 91).

The emergence of the client as active self-healer in psychotherapy out-come research is a development that I have much welcomed, not least because it supports the basis of my own approach to practice! This emphasis places the client back at the centre of the change process where he belongs, and begins to honour some of those client factors that are active in psychotherapeutic change such as the client's innate self-actualizing capacity and his readiness to engage in this type of interpersonal learning, long a part of humanistic approaches and cer-tainly a factor that attracted me from the early 1960s when I first 'met' psychotherapy as a process. The client who is motivated to change will often make the best of what is on offer and use those aspects of the method employed by the therapist that she finds useful and compatible with her expectations and simply ignore what is not useful. I remind myself that I do well to sacrifice my theories when challenged in this way, rather than my clients!

The word 'integrative' in the title of this chapter refers to an ongoing process of personal and professional learning that I have experienced as I practise as a psychotherapist, because, like many of my colleagues, I share a tendency to use 'what works' and to integrate into my personal style aspects of different approaches and techniques I see or read about almost without being aware of the gradual change in my overall style of working. In this way, I have moved further and further away from the pure-form approach of my original training, a finding that has been long supported by research (Fiedler, 1950). For me, this has involved integrat-ing into my style of working a view of unconscious processes as these play out in everyday life and so also in the therapeutic relationship. Whatever the problem is for the client 'out there', she is likely to reproduce this troublesome process in the context of the therapeutic relationship where there will be an opportunity to work this through in the safety and containment of the therapy room. In this way, the material for therapy involves the emergence in the here-and-now immediacy of the encounter between therapist and client of patterns of behaviour and unconscious communications that may be troublesome for the client in her everyday life. These can then be worked with in different ways in the present. As Yalom points out, if a client wishes to change a maladaptive pattern that is interfering with her relationships out in the world, the therapist needs to be alert to the replay of the pattern in the therapeutic encounter which then provides material for discussion. For example, a client who was complaining of a tendency to please others and adapt to her demands and expectations of her suddenly stopped in midstream and said: 'Even here I am constantly working out how to be the best client for you.' The way she was hearing and interpreting my comments and responding to non-verbal behaviours then became the fruitful therapeutic material. As Yalom (2001, p. 52) puts this, 'the general strategy is to find *a here-and-now equivalent* of the dysfunctional interaction. Once this is done, the work becomes much more accurate and immediate'. Like Yalom, my preference is to work with the immediacy of what is happening in the room which is a focus that existentialism and humanism have in common.

However, it is always important to remember that clients may be unconsciously communicating to the therapist emotional experiences out of their present awareness which they may never have put into words and may carry in body memories and disjointed pictures or images only. My task as therapist then becomes to assist clients in gradually accessing and putting words to sensations, feelings, images and experiences that may never have been put into language before. Casement (1985) uses the term 'communication by impact' to describe the process when clients behave in such a way 'that they stir up feelings in the therapist which could not be communicated in words'. Casement (1985, p. 72) further makes the point that the clients may be communicating their experience to the therapist in the only way that they are currently able to do, and that the therapist may need to hold or tolerate these feelings until clients are ready to deal with them and assimilate them into their narrative. He believes that clients may re-create in the therapist the kind of attitude towards themselves that their parents may have had, so that we as therapists need to monitor our feelings carefully and in this process may gain valuable information about the client's experience in the world and with people. What is important is that we 'note' these feelings but do not 'act into' them, otherwise we may well re-enact the original trauma for the client. Premature self-disclosure of my own responses may have a similar impact on the client. I have gradually learned, too, that premature confrontation may have a deleterious effect on the therapy and I have (sometimes regretfully and with some nostalgia) resisted the impulse to leap in with some of the more vigorous techniques I learnt in my original gestalt and transactional analysis training!

However, in the context of a humanistic approach that privileges the real relationship, appropriate self-disclosure, for example, may be a powerful intervention. In this way the authentic person of the therapist is brought directly into the therapeutic encounter. On occasion, sharing with a client how his story impacts on me as another human being can be a powerful confirmation for the client of his feelings of pain or humiliation in a traumatic relationship. I may also, at times, share my own response to a client's familiar pattern of interacting with people in order to give her feedback about her impact on another person, so that she can assimilate this information in the process of change.

My most powerful learning in the past decade has come from refining the manner in which I 'listen' to a client's conscious and unconscious communications to inform my interventions. I have come to realize, more and more, that to talk of rules that define what is 'right' and what is 'wrong' in therapy and the prescription of correct procedures may well do violence to the here-and-now encounter between me and my client. Some of the rules that were impressed on me years ago such as 'never give advice' or 'confront, confront, confront dysfunctional behaviour' led me into paths that I now regret. I have felt impressed and supported by two recent contributions to the practice of psychotherapy, the first by the existentialist Yalom (2001) and the second by the psychoanalyst Casement (2002), who both emphasize the central importance of attending to the ongoing process of the work and not sacrificing this sensitive attention to process for an adherence to rules and procedures. This honouring of the therapeutic relationship in all its unique complexity sits very well with me!

Chapter 21
When the world changes: one humanistic perspective of transpersonal psychotherapy

COURTENAY YOUNG

Alongside, or perhaps even as part of, the realm of humanistic psychology, there is another mainstream branch of psychology or psychotherapy called 'transpersonal psychology' and there is a considerable overlap between these two branches. Transpersonal psychology was a later development to attempt to integrate ideas about identity previously embodied in religious practice that had been ignored in the prevailing theories of psychoanalysis and behaviourism. The idea of the self as an entity that develops through a journey and that is grounded in something bigger is a key part of this innovation.

> Maslow's ideas about self-actualization, Jung's ideas about archetypes and the collective unconscious . . . are all important in transpersonal psychology. Guided fantasy and other methods, especially ones involving symbols, are used to explore them (Jones, 1994).

But I feel that this does not give a proper and full description of the reality of transpersonal psychology, as I experience it as a practitioner in the field. So I want to approach this from the other end of a spectrum that has a slightly more personal spiritual perspective, and which is also very experiential. I call it 'when the world changes'. This end of the field can be extreme and dramatic. This perspective is also quite pragmatic because these aspects are often what I actually work with. This end of the spectrum considers an essential part of humanistic psychology and psychotherapy to be concerned with a human being's actual spiritual growth and transformation, and this is not just an inclusion of the realm of the spirit (along with the mind and body), but is based on actual experiences. This process carries its own unique set of rules.

The death of what is commonly called 'the ego' is often necessary before spirit can fully emerge into the human psyche. And it can seem as if parts of us, sometimes the older familial 'stuff' or even karmic patterns, have to be left behind, to die, or even to be destroyed (depending on how deeply we identify with our egos or our histories) before we can more fully live according to our human potential. This is almost inevitably a very painful process and it can also be terrifying if we do not happen to realize what is happening to us. Spiritual growth does not happen just from wish fulfilment. Many of us are searching for something better, for something beyond that which we can see, touch or feel in our everyday lives. We often use phrases like, 'I am looking for some meaning to my life.' 'I want to develop my sense of self.' Many of us, to begin with, do not know what that 'something' is. We may use the word 'spirit' in this context. This word, however, is often used without really knowing what it means, or what it contains. It also seems that this form of spiritual development is beginning to happen more spontaneously in people as well, as a phenomenon, and not as a result of their searching. And this is where my work comes in.

I am becoming aware of an increasingly general and widespread awakening of spirit. Not only do people want to connect their personal process with their transpersonal, or find different and better ways of doing what they do already but with more meaning, more essence, and more spirit – and the joy and grace that comes with spirit – but also people are beginning to find, quite suddenly and sometimes quite frighteningly, that they are having spontaneous spiritual or transpersonal experiences. I call these types of experience this because (a) there is no other appropriate description and (b) that is what I think they are.

Let me use an analogy of a society that does not recognize puberty as a healthy stage of human development. The dramatic changes in female body shape in the early teenage years are thus distortions. The growth of hair on the face, under the arms and in the pubic area are also aberrations and considered disgusting. There is something wrong with the change in a man's voice. And so they have discovered surgical techniques and pharmaceutical remedies to correct these deformations. Adolescent spots mean a skin disease; we have lotions. 'Puppy-fat' is corrected by rigid dieting. Some people reject adolescence 'naturally' and become anorexic – which is seen as a good thing, rather than an illness. The symptoms of puberty and adolescence become so condemned and vilified that people experiencing these feel shameful, and the person ends up being rejected by society.

I suggest that this is what we do with the 'normal' human spiritual developmental processes that should happen as 'naturally' and 'easily' as a healthy adolescence. This spiritual emergence process tends to happen in a person's more mature years, often somewhere between 30 and 40. Our investments of staying as we are and not developing differently are much more rigid then. We have jobs, mortgages, families, a 'position' in life, and so forth – as if spirit cared!

So these experiences and the symptoms that attach themselves to such emerging experiences are thus often misunderstood. Not everybody is aware of spiritual dimensions or open to seeing psychological and transpersonal processes in this light. Quite frequently the actual manifest-ations of spiritual awakening are, and have been, mistaken for symptoms of psychosis, or insanity, or witchcraft, or demonic possession, or illness. Let me give an example. An elderly lady in Texas rang up a referral service some years ago and said, 'Can you help me? Last Christmas God came and sat on my head.' When asked what she meant by that, she said, 'I seem to know things that are going to happen before they happen and I get messages telling me what to do and what is happening with other people. I know what people are thinking.' Then she went on to say: 'Now, my Minister says that I am of the Devil and my women's group say that I am a witch, and my husband, well, he just doesn't want to know anything about this at all, so can you help me?' Her problem was not her process (it was like God coming and sitting in her head) but in the reactions of the people around her.

The results of what seem like a spiritual journey or process are some-times as devastating to the person involved, or to those around them, as a serious illness can be or the death of that person would be. In some cases they are more devastating. The transformational processes are not considered as part of normal reality, and the 'loved one' therefore becomes abnormal. So when someone becomes involved in such a process, nobody knows how to handle it: there isn't a language, a road map, a set of concepts: there is just an aberration.

I mentioned the concept of the death of the ego and leaving behind some of the personal processes being a necessary part of spiritual matur-ation. This, in one form or another, is acknowledged by nearly every religion, including the twentieth-century Western religion of psychology. Sometimes it is expressed as surrender; sometimes as an initiation; some-times as a purging of the old; sometimes as a taking on of the new – like a marriage. It is nearly always described as a major transformation of and for the individual. It is sometimes taken seriously – within a religious con-text. But if it transgresses the bounds of that religion or if the symptoms do not fit with the practices of that religion, or the person becomes scared and irrational, then that person is often abandoned. Nobody wants to know. And this makes the situation worse. These people become the 'lepers' of society, or exorcism (nowadays called 'spiritual deliverance') is called for.

If a society does not facilitate this maturational spiritual transformation with some rite of passage, or acknowledge it with respect, or plan for it, or expect it, or welcome it in any way whatsoever, individuals are then not only struggling with their own personal processes in realms with which they are often unfamiliar, but they are also struggling with the (active) resistance of the conservative collective process. That response may be to incarcerate people in mental asylums because (for example) they think they are hearing the voice of God, or whatever. This has happened fre-quently over the years, and is still happening, although usually for shorter periods of time. Psychotropic medication is often used extensively as well.

I do not believe that people are becoming psychotic in these processes, although this can happen briefly; however they may be becoming increasingly psychic and the significant point is that the manifestations are often quite similar.

Furthermore, the family of the individual often feels that this loved person has become strange, alien or remote. That person is much less concerned with what has been the medium by which the family has bound itself together. They no longer do that which is expected. The person, the 'loved one', has changed. There is a sort of betrayal here. Love is supposed to be 'happily ever after' – at least we are told so often enough. It is a short step from this change in love, to that person being alienated from the close family and thus the support that they may need in order to go through this change. In some cases the alienation is total and it is as if the person has indeed died.

The person's actual experience can be very, very different: totally 'off beam'. It can feel as if such people, for the first time, are truly alive. They see more; understand more; are intensely aware of everything around them. It can be, and often is, euphoric. This is the fantastic part – "At last I have 'made it'; 'I truly understand'". But if you can't make others understand; if they don't want to know what you have become aware of, or are experiencing; if your experience is outside of their limitations or constructs; then the pleasure soon turns to pain, the elation to terror, and the euphoria to despair, and the transpersonal episode can easily become a psychotic one.

Stan and Christina Grof (1991) have identified various forms of spiritual emergency. Awakening of the Kundalini (serpent power) is where there is a radical transformation of people's relationship with their biology. There are often powerful physical sensations: heat, streaming energy, tremors, violent shaking, spasms, violent twistings. Extreme illnesses and sometimes childbirth can bring on such experiences, or are a result of it. The symptoms can also be mistaken for epilepsy. A shamanic journey is often accompanied by a dramatic episode involving an altered state of consciousness. There is an emphasis on physical suffering and encounter with death followed by rebirth and elements of ascent. A psychological renewal through activation of a central archetype is where people perceive themselves in some form or other as being in the middle of a world process and again there are elements of death, afterlife and return to the beginnings. The form of the experience lends itself to interpretation of a central archetype experience. A psychic opening is an episode characterized by striking instances of extrasensory perception (ESP) and other parapsychological manifestations – like the little lady in Texas. An emergence of a karmic pattern is where the individual might experience dramatic events that seem to be connected to a past lifetime or birth, and where there is a flavour of a different time or spatial context. Possession is where the person might take on facial characteristics, gestures and attitudes of something typically diabolic in nature. This does not mean that they are actually possessed by an outside agency that is evil but that the pattern of spirit emerging through them in a disturbed way (possibly distorted by the history or belief systems) seems to take on this form. There seems little doubt that such experiences occur.

There are many other types of transformative spiritual experience: Christina Grof (1991) states that alcoholism is often a distorted search for the wrong sort of 'spirit'. Major illnesses, including a genuine psychotic episode, and major traumas or accidents are also often significant triggers for people to go into a radical process of spiritual change. Some people experience a sudden conversion to an established religion. There are cultural and social forces at work, driving people towards or away from their spiritual lives; some of these seem to be fundamentalist, others have more equanimity. Some cultures have ritual initiations that provide the (necessary?) shock to start a person's psyche growing and working. For others, it is moving to a new culture and having many of one's old assumptions disturbed as they come into contact with the new and different values and moralities. Burnout, experienced when you have done all that you physically and emotionally can and it is still not enough, can be a gateway for some to the new set of resources, hidden deep within and contactable only in desperation when all else has failed. For some, it is a contact with nature or aspects of the natural environment that trigger this greater and deeper awareness. Finally, our very human capacity to create wars, survive major disasters, experience earthquakes and the like, can also create the conditions to bring out the best in those around us in such events. These people are touched by their heroism: it is their unsought gateway to a new and richer life.

What, I believe, is necessary is to validate all these different forms of spiritual experiences, more and more often. DSM IV, the diagnostic manual for psychiatrists, now mentions a spiritual crisis among its categories. This is just one brick in the wall. As a juxtaposition, Caroline Myss, a spiritual clairvoyant, once said to me: 'Never doubt that you have a personal Guardian Angel. It is part of the package of being human.' The possibility of a rich spiritual life is part of our human birthright and we need culturally to reclaim this part of the package and start to live our lives more fully.

Transpersonal psychology is just another set of tools and concepts to help people handle this human life: as monasteries are impractical and austere nowadays and the mystery schools are long gone. The ordinary person in the street, experiencing some of the richness and weirdness of their Inner Life needs to be able to talk to people about it: people who are well grounded in some of the dynamics of a spiritual life. Gurus and transcendental masters still exist, and they are also human; open to temptation; and their way is not necessarily yours. What many people need is a guide who guides from behind; a transpersonal psychotherapist should be able to do this. This way of working emerged out of humanistic psychology and its client-centred, process-oriented ways of working, but with this extra in-depth perspective or focus on our inner life.

If, as I believe, there is a new pattern or phase of human growth happening, which is that of a spiritual nature, then we, as a race or a global culture, need to recognize and prepare for it. In exactly the same way that we create rites of passage or initiations for adulthood, marriage and to some extent death, we also need to begin to develop these for spiritual growth or emergence. This awakening, perhaps more than any other factor, carries with it the hope that we shall not obliterate ourselves as a species and a planet with either a bang or a whimper; that there is something greater than ourselves of which we are an intrinsic part – you may call this God if you wish – and that, however frightening or disturbing these processes may seem, they are part of a healthy growth and need to be recognized as such.

Some of the main modalities or types of transpersonal psychotherapy that can be found in existence today are various types of psychosynthesis (Assagioli), core process psychotherapy (Karuna, UK), core energetics (Pierrakos), and transpersonal psychotherapy (Gordon-Brown and Somers, UK); and the Institute of Transpersonal Psychotherapy (Menlo Park, California); transpersonally psychotherapeutic teachings and growth work based on Hindu, Zen or Buddhist philosophies (such as Ram Das, Da Free John, Bagwan, Sai Baba, Deepak Chopra, Thich Naht Hahn); the work of Ken Wilber; some of the psychotherapy workshops found at places like Esalen, California; the Open Centre and the Omega Institute (in and near New York), and the Findhorn Foundation in Scotland, amongst many others. Recent developments in Arnie Mindell's Process Oriented Psychotherapy; Stanislav Grof's methods of Holotropic Breathwork; aspects of Ron Kurtz's work in Hakomi; much of Bob Moore's work; some aspects of primal integration (especially when combined with Frank Lake's work on clinical theology); astrological counselling; some shamanistic or some native American therapies; soul retrieval therapy, and those using concepts from paganism or wicca, also overlap considerably into this field of thought and practice called collectively transpersonal psychology or psychotherapy. But all this tells us nothing about the actual content of transpersonal psychotherapy.

Transpersonal psychology, in my view, is relatively empty and meaningless without some of the richness of these emergences, and emergencies. Many of the founders of branches of transpersonal psychology, mentioned earlier, have had such experiences. In trying to understand these for themselves, perhaps they have given us forms, concepts and structures that help us move in similar directions; and perhaps they have softened out some of the bumps in the road. And again, these are just modern-day road maps: the actual territory is different.

What seems to be happening is something much more basic; something that comes from or relates to the very core of our humanity, our spirits, our souls. Maybe it is this that makes us different from other animals. I don't know. They don't seem to have such a struggle, and such a perspective could also be a form of anthropomorphic fascism. But if we do have spirits; if the movement of energy within our souls is to mature during our human existence then when does this happen, how does this happen, and how can we help it to happen? As humanistic psychotherapists, we need more answers and I firmly believe that some of the answers lie within this particular perspective.

PART FIVE
PRESENT SITUATIONS AND FUTURE DIRECTIONS

Chapter 22
The place of humanistic psychotherapy today

Where is humanistic psychotherapy now? Is it so deeply connected to an age of change that has now passed that it is no longer relevant? Has the human potential movement ended? Are we left with a distillation of its ideals into a profession that, by its very nature, is antipathetic to its origins? What was happening for a lot of people when the movement began was a genuine search for an alternative to the restrictions of fossilized authoritarian middle-class values, which insisted on rules that had the effect of not trusting people to know what was best for themselves. It established the client clearly in charge of the therapy. It espoused a belief that people come first and systems second. This was in contradiction to the then-current use of psychology for political and commercial ends. Humanistic therapy today exists in what has been described as the 'audit society' in which 'the dominant style of managerialism is derived from accountancy' (Prichett and Erskine-Hill, 2002, pp. 16–17). Has the humanistic approach changed its role as a critique of existing norms or has it succumbed to contemporary norms, or have those norms changed under the influence of the humanistic movement so that it has now served its original purpose and taken a more central part in the process of change? These are the questions that are addressed in the final part of this book.

What has changed?

- The majority of people coming into therapy are no longer looking for a counterculture but the resolution of ordinary everyday problems without necessarily wishing to change their way of life. In my experience, and that of my colleagues, the range of social and ethnic backgrounds has changed. Those who formerly would have had an aversion to therapy, particularly any type that may be emotionally or physically directed, now come with a readiness to explore themselves in depth. Maybe they come more problem centred than the client population of earlier years. However, they are not so easy to put into a social grouping.

155

- Professional practice has moved a long way since the origins of the human potential movement. The setting up of systems of control – no doubt in the best interests of the public – limits the independence of therapists. True, there need to be professional standards and guidelines. It is important for any professional to be accountable. We all make mistakes, but it is counter to the spirit of humanistic therapy that outside bodies are the main arbiter of what is good. Standards of initial training and continuing development have become more demanding.
- Psychotherapy is much more accessible. Many medical practices have counsellors on their staff. (53% in 1999). Counselling is available and sometimes paid for by corporations, businesses and public authorities such as the police. I have been involved in setting up clinical supervision for nurses, which provides person-centred support for staff. Although the spread of counselling has enabled working relations in organizations to be more humanistic, it can be used to keep people calm and in line with aims of the organization.
- Humanistic values have probably become more circumstantial. The moral and spiritual imperatives that motivated the prime movers of the growth movement have given way to more down-to-earth issues such as professional survival. It was necessary for the free-spirited origins to be more grounded in the everyday concerns of maintenance in order to continue.

Many of those who were my contemporaries 20 years ago were free from responsibilities. Few were married or owned property. Many had no status to worry about professionally or socially – either because they didn't have any or had left it to pursue their higher aims. Now most of my colleagues do have the responsibilities of family and/or paying a mortgage and need to maintain a practice in a way that only a few were bothered about 25 years ago. Practitioners have become more respectable. This is not necessarily a bad thing and certainly nothing to grieve over. 'The times they are a'changing' and many have moved with them. What we have now is a loosely knit group of schools that would place themselves under the umbrella of humanistic psychotherapy. It would be unrealistic and unfair to make any assessment of how any of these has changed from its origins in the growth movement. To the best of my knowledge they are still encouraging experiment, promoting autonomy, trusting the process of self-regulation and welcoming diversity.

What is the present place of humanistic psychotherapy in the context of contemporary society and in the field of psychotherapy and health practice? There are many more therapists in the humanistic field than ever, due to the expansion of training agencies. These work in a wide variety of settings – in private practice, in the health service, in education, social work, the prison service, churches. So the enterprise is thriving in many aspects. Undoubtedly, the humanistic movement has affected the way in which people deal with each other both in institutions and the community. Most of the methods used in human relations training in the world of business customer relations and management training have been derived from humanistic methods. This has become almost a business on its own. True, in the long run, it is for monetary ends, but the message 'people are important' has become well established. It may be worthwhile noting that making money is not unhumanistic. It is the misuse of power to control people that is the moral issue. Although for a time left-wing activists aligned themselves with the alternative movement, it was to fight against the overpowering use of technology by the big corporations as exposed by Vance Packard in *Hidden Persuaders* (1957) and described with flair by Theodore Roszak (1971) in *The Making of a Counter Culture*.

Most importantly, changes effected by humanistic practice were to be seen in the family therapy movement in the USA, which was responsible for the publication of the *Family Therapy Networker*, a monthly periodical started in 1982 at the height of the growth movement and which has included in its purview the work of a large number of radical thinkers and practitioners including Salvador Minuchin, Carl Whitaker, Ronnie Laing, Virginia Satir, Thomas Szasz, Jay Haley, Milton Erickson, and many others who have been the shapers of family therapy in America and who were part of the outpouring of the alternative approach to therapy. However, by the 1990s this revolutionary fringe movement started by a bunch of rebels went respectably and successfully mainstream (*Networker*, January/February 1992). As health care plans and insurance boomed, so the therapy generally became more litigious and restrictive in regulating the professions.

Now that humanistic psychotherapy has become more mainstream, has it lost some its unique impact and idealism at the door of respectability? Its voice as a moral alternative has been somewhat subdued. As noted earlier, the advances in standards for practising have largely been beneficial to the service offered but although this may be reassuring for many, most people today would not know the difference between what was being offered then in a setup that was more self-regulatory and the authoritative regulation that is now in place.

The UK Association of Humanistic Psychology Practitioners (UKAHPP) has taken a middle line. Since its inception in 1980 it has sought to establish high professional standards based on humanistic principles. It was one of the main contributors to the setting up of the Standing Conference for Psychotherapy in 1989, which later became UK Council for Psychotherapy (UKCP). This association accredits psychotherapists, counsellors and other practitioners in a wide range of categories. Without having any vested interest in any one method, it has sought to give support and backing to those practitioners who have either a wide range of training or who do not ally themselves with any one body of therapeutic training or practice. So although it has espoused the registration route it still maintains a certain amount of independence.

Although there is an increasingly recognized move to establish human-istic practice in the world of psychotherapy at large, this takes different forms. The large majority of therapists are not registered and may be seen by some as operating in a kind of limbo. This does not make them any less dedicated or competent. It may be that some do not have sufficient train-ing or that some have undergone considerable training but do not choose to go the route of becoming registered. They may have their own network of support, assessment and supervision. This is certainly true of those who are members of the Independent Practitioners Network (IPN), which was set up in opposition to the UKCP. This is organized on a completely different basis. It is self-regulatory, with a network of groups that carry out self- and peer assessment. It is worth noting here the Open Centre is a multidisciplinary co-operative. The Open Centre has been established since 1977 and upheld the original vision of the growth movement of being both inclusive and yet clearly independent in its approach to pro-viding a service based on collaboration and choice. It has practitioners from a range of disciplines who do not necessarily agree or work in the same way, but all have the objective of treating their clients in an equal and growthful way. A similar organization is Spectrum, which has been functioning for a long time as a centre of humanistic practice, although it is not organized on a co-operative basis.

Groups

As has already been noted in Part One, one of the distinguishing features of the human growth movement was the widespread use of group work. Although groups are still used by many humanistic therapists, their preva-lence seems to have diminished. According to Guy Gladstone (2002), only five out of 27 practitioners listing themselves as humanistic group thera-pists were running groups. This confirms the general impression that groups are no longer the hallmark of humanistic practice. The possible reasons for this trend are the difficulty of maintaining ongoing groups due to the cost of suitable premises; a reduced demand from the general public; lack of skills, both in organizing and running a group; that groups are too demanding for the therapist; the preference by clients for the priv-acy of individual therapy; and a fear of exposure to others who are not as safe. Alongside this, it is true to say that, with some notable exceptions, most of the training courses in psychotherapy do not provide training in group work. Although most use groups as means of training, the output is directed to one-to-one practice. Therefore, this is the expectation that graduates take with them. As I mentioned in the section on training, it would be beneficial for all trainees in humanistic psychotherapy to have an ongoing and/or intensive experience of group work outside the con-fines of the training agency. It is possible, however, that there are just as many groups operating, but fewer compared with the increasing number of practitioners since the early 1990s.

All this, of course, presupposes that group therapy has an equal place alongside individual therapy. It is my contention that in many ways group therapy is a more enriching and growthful arena for change than individual therapy. It provides an environment that more closely resembles relationships outside therapy. People experience a range of different responses in addition to the therapist and a group setting discourages over-dependence on the therapist. It gives people the freedom to learn from the work of others on their problems, and some comfort that they are not alone in their dilemmas. They can be as active as they wish. They do not have to fill the whole of an hour's session by themselves. Groups also have the advantage of providing a wide range of experience in a safe environment. Many people have a problem in relating to others freely in their lives and the group acts as a workshop to experiment with expression of feelings and behaviour. It is also an alternative place to deal with the inherent alienation in society, the break up of families, and the increasing competitiveness of working and social life. Comparatively, individual therapy could be seen as finding in the therapist that special relationship which was missing in childhood. In groups you get both that and peer support.

It is true that groups are demanding for the therapist and initially for the members, but the rewards and outcomes for both are potentially much greater. It is also true that there is a wide range of styles of group work, but most group therapists arrange for an initial interview to deal with these issues. There are also a number of one-off weekend groups which give anyone a chance to sample the 'flavour'. There are still a number of centres that offer a programme of groups – notably the Open Centre, Spectrum and Metanoia.

Spreading the limits

What is clear is that, since the late 1980s or early 1990s, many of the ideas and methods of humanistic practice have spread into areas that are not clearly identified as being humanistic. The influence of the humanistic movement of the 1960s has been felt without necessarily being distinguished. This is because of those who have recognized the more fruitful ways of working laid out by the humanistic movement, which may have been passed on to them second or third hand and have become normative without any clear label. In almost every area of professional life, including the mainstream world of counselling and therapy, you can see hints of the values of humanistic psychology. Outside of this, there have been considerable changes in practice, from the shop floor to the consulting room. Now there is an emphasis on responding to people's needs rather than deciding what is good for them or what might be politically acceptable. Focus groups have become a norm for political parties and commercial enterprises. The phrase 'retail therapy' has crept into everyday language. This may be seen as a move towards consumer power, but it is close to putting people first – the basis of humanistic belief. It may be debatable as to whether we live in a more egalitarian society, but there has been an evolution in the way that people's inner motivation and desire to grow have been acknowledged. It cannot, of course, be claimed that all these improvements in people work are due to the humanistic movement, but the genesis of the change of attitude in training and practice in these fields is attributable to the ethos of the alternative movement in which humanistic therapy played a significant part.

In the more immediate field of human growth, there has been the burgeoning, since the early 1990s, of what is known as 'New Age' activity. Although it includes a wide range of 'therapies', it is hard to distinguish these in places from more normative psychotherapeutic practices. They have a clearly spiritual texture and, although many of them have been effective in healing and growth, many have a non-scientific basis, some quite deliberately. Many of those who were and still are part of the humanistic movement have decamped into this territory, which has the benefit of being outside the restrictions of mainstream practice. There is a lot of overlap between New Age ideology and humanistic psychology, particularly in the positive attitude to the universe, the belief in the oneness of humanity, a 'holistic' model of life that views the world as a living organism with its parts indivisibly related, the recognition of a spiritual dimension in human experience.

Alongside this, there is the increasingly widespread use of *complementary medicine*. Many are derived from other cultural sources but include many well-established practices such as massage, aromatherapy, shiastu, reflexology. The annual festival of holistic living offers a shop window for the whole spectrum of alternative approaches to healing, health and growth. These all make various claims, which, for the most part, are outside the realms of humanistic psychotherapy and yet offer a parallel alternative route to finding peace and enlightenment.

Without making any attempt to cover this field of endeavour here, it is clear that much of the ground of the humanistic movement has been absorbed into the New Age arena outside of the constraints of the professional practice of psychotherapy. Consequently, this is beyond the limitations of this book. Some would argue that, as the schools of humanistic psychology have become more conventional, New Age followers have taken up the alternative role in society. There are many paths through life and whatever helps people on their journey is to be welcomed. At the same time it is necessary to recognize that there needs to be some caution in this whole area. The dilemma is that, whereas humanistic psychology encourages people to choose for themselves, there needs to be some guidance and reference point to avoid fraud. I have heard of people who feel that they have been cheated and not helped by those claiming to provide 'cures'. I also know of a lot of people who have benefited from the influence of alternative forms of healing.

The other major development is the *conservation movement*. Many of the ideals of the growth movement have inspired this worldwide endeavour to preserve life on our planet. Concerns about the quality of life, the resistance to technology, multinational greed, and pollution generally, have extended the values of the humanistic movement related to people to the natural and material environment we inhabit. The widespread involvement of people at all levels would have been unthinkable a generation ago. This growing interest in the welfare of the earth is a natural outcome of the values of humanistic psychology. It is the context of putting people alongside all living creatures first. It is the recognition that we are mutually dependent and responsible for *how* we live.

The future

There seem to be three possible directions for humanistic psychotherapy. One is that it will continue be a definable and serious force in the therapy field and beyond, with an emphasis on unity within diversity. The second is that it will be consumed into the general maelstrom of psychotherapy, leaving a minority of independent practitioners who will call themselves something else – educators, facilitators, life coaches and so forth. The third is that there will be an increasing amount of training and practice that will be integrative and not based in any particular discipline, so that individual methods will cease to have such a clear separate identity.

In the USA a large number of humanistic professionals have become incorporated into the American Psychological Association in a way that seemed unthinkable in the mid-1970s, and they have had an impact on the revision of its policy. In *The Handbook of Humanistic Psychology* (Schneider et al., 2001), produced by the American Association of Humanistic Psychology, there seems to be an emphasis on this direction for humanistic psychology, in order to have a greater impact on the wider world of psychotherapy. In Europe, the humanistic endeavour is mainly sponsored by the European Association for Psychotherapy. In the UK it is now a clear and strong element in the Humanistic and Integrative Section (HIPS) of UKCP, of which the UKAHPP is an active member body. But that is only what is happening at an organizational level.

What is more significant is that the practice of humanistic psychotherapy may not need such a definitive profile, but those who endorse its values will continue to maintain them as part of their own personal and professional development. It is more important that what the humanistic movement stands for is perpetuated, rather than any label. The reality is that a name or a structure is probably the best means of continuing and extending its influence, not only in the world of therapy but in the wider realms of social, commercial and political endeavour.

The Handbook of Humanistic Psychology (Schneider et al., 2001), produced by the American Association of Humanistic Psychology suggests that, in the USA at least, the movement is still vibrant and identifiable. Over 60 writers, practitioners and teachers were gathered from a wide spectrum of methodologies to produce a contemporary picture of the way in which humanistic psychology has developed. It is very impressive, covering such a wide range of subjects as gender issues, ecology, peace, the arts, research, managed care, education, body/mind medicine, social action, romanticism and morality. The general drift is that the future of humanistic psychology lies in gaining a stronger voice academically and scientifically in mainstream psychology and developing respectability for transpersonal psychology. In the closing statements one of the editors, Kirk Schneider, writes:

> To sum, humanistic psychology, as Taylor put it so succinctly, is at a crossroads, but so is the profession that inspired it. The question is, will these fields find ways in which to cooperate, to transcend their parochialism, and to link their traditions, or will they continue to clash, to go their separate ways, and to further subject the profession to impoverishment and eventual co-optation? For humanistic psychology, this question rides on two essential tracks: the willingness to bolster its scholarly output and the willingness to further articulate its scientific perspective (particularly as it relates to social policy). For organized psychology, the question is one of integrity. Will organized psychology return to its original (humanistic) inquiries (what does it mean to be fully experientially human, and how does that understanding illuminate the vital or fulfilled life?), or will it be co-opted by current fashions (e.g., biologism, technicism, nihilism) and atrophy as a result?
>
> I hope that we have shown in this volume that a full and human psychology is an experiential psychology, a psychology that embraces all dimensions of human awareness and subawareness but particularly those that have meaning, impact, and significance for each given person. The challenge is to articulate that meaningful resonance to weave out of it a rich and subtly nuanced theory, philosophy, or guideline – and to apply that understanding to a diverse and hungering populace. This is a populace that has been bombarded by cosmetic fixes but that yearns, I believe, for existential sustenance. (2001, p. 673)

Many of those who were part of the humanistic movement saw it as a political force, not in any organisational way but by practising in such a manner that is personal, subjective and based on experience. The signs are that this imperative, though still present, has waned. Roszak (1981) believed that the major need for mankind is to recover the sense of the personal – the politics of the person. Many of my peers became involved in therapy not because they wanted to do good or be fashionable or become rich or achieve status and power, although these motives were no doubt present, but because in doing this work they could be involved in something that made sense and gave authenticity to their experience, and because they believed they were involved in something that could and did make profound changes in people's lives and society at large. 'Whether we like it or not, the decision to be a therapist is also a commitment to our own growth' (Kottler, 1990 pp. ix–x). This they found for themselves in humanistic therapy, groups and communities. This way of practising has the integrity to combat inauthentic behaviour, mechanistic and impersonal forms of dealing with people as entities. The very close encounter in the therapeutic relationship is an antidote to what Roszak (1981) calls 'the myth of objective consciousness' in which 'the mechanistic imperative has been successfully internalised as the prevailing life style of our society' (p. 231).

Without necessarily becoming actively involved in politics, it must be recognized that psychotherapy is a profoundly political activity in itself. The humanistic approach is consciously practising a personalistic lifestyle. Of course, we as therapists are concerned about the big issues of our times, but what we are doing, day by day, is helping people to make sense of their lives and change them so that they are more human, more personal in their dealings with themselves and others, which is just as important a contribution to changing the world.

Personal epilogue

It is this conviction that fuels the enterprise in which I am involved, called the humanistic movement – that it is in the best sense alternative, that it questions the so-called norms of society when they are denying the essential nature of human beings, at the same time ensuring that the professional practice of psychotherapy does not become overidentified with these norms so that it becomes a business more than a practice.

My aim in writing this book as been to portray in broad strokes the essence of the humanistic approach to psychotherapy for the benefit of those who are interested, mystified, or those who have never heard of it. My fear is that humanistic psychotherapy can become so rarefied and mystifying that it gives the impression of being accessible or available only to a certain breed of people who can comprehend the complexities / complex processes of psychology or, at worst, to those who have to be so needy that they will not mind.

One of the aims of Eric Berne, the founder of transactional analysis, was to produce a language about personality and relationships that could be understood by an 8-year-old. As a tribute to this, one of the questions in the transactional analysis qualifying exam was based on this assumption. That may be seen as simplistic and naive, but perhaps we have to become little again in order to comprehend ourselves and others better.

It is great to have the learning and the power to help to influence people for their good. Most of us would accept that. It also carries with it the responsibility to be as straightforward as possible – to avoid setting ourselves up as experts on other people rather to help ourselves and the people we serve to see what *is* rather than what we think is. That, for me, is the legacy of the humanistic movement, whose leaders were highly intelligent and also had the desire, will and ability to make direct contact creatively with people. Human experience does not fit neatly into packages. Each individual is unique and sees, hears and feels the world in their own way. Being human and relating to other humans is recognizing that and cherishing it. There is an enormous amount of suffering experienced by people in this modern world. Much of it is caused by forces outside of us. There is a lot that we create from within. While we all want to resist the evil forces around us, we first need to look inside ourselves. From that self-knowledge we shall be able to see more clearly what requires our attention in the world.

It is my hope that humanistic psychotherapy will continue to be open and accessible to the public, that it will be less concerned about its own internal structure and more concerned with getting on with the job of being with the people who come for help, so that it avoids the condemnation of a former Archbishop of Canterbury who said of the Anglican Church that it was so busy repairing the boat that it never put to sea! The great achievement of the humanistic movement was that it took psychotherapy out of the closet and moved it out into the social milieu of its time. In our time this may take on a different form, but the spirit of the humanistic enterprise can still remain a powerful force as the leaven in the lump!

References

Assagioli R (1975) Psychosynthesis: A Manual of Principles and Techniques. London: Turnstone Press

Assagioli R (1984) The Act of Will. New York: HarperCollins.

Batten TR (1967) The Non-directive Approach in Group and Community Work. London: Oxford University Press.

Beisser A (1970) The Paradoxical Theory of Change. In J Fagan, I Sheperd (eds) Gestalt Therapy Now, Theory/Techniques/Applications. New York: Harper & Row.

Berne E (1961) Transactional Analysis in Psychotherapy. London: Souvenir Press.

Berne E (1966). Principles of Group Treatment. New York: Grove Press.

Berne E (1947/1957) A Layman's Guide to Psychiatry and Psychoanalysis. New York: Grove Press.

Berne E (1961) Transactional Analysis in Psychotherapy. New York: Ballantine Books.

Berne E (1972) What Do You Say After You Say Hello? London: Corgi Books.

Bernstein B, Lecomte C (1981) Licensure in psychology: alternative directions. Professional Psychology 12: 200–8.

Boadella D (1973) Wilhelm Reich: The Evolution of his Work. London: Arcana.

Boadella, D (1987). Lifestreams – An Introduction to Biosynthesis. London: Routledge & Kegan Paul.

Bradford JP, Gibb JR, Benne KD (1964) T-group and Laboratory Method. New York: John Wiley & Sons.

Bragan K (1996) Self and Spirit in the Therapeutic Relationship. London: Routledge.

Buber M (1970) I and Thou. New York: Simon & Schuster.

Campbell J (1976) Occidental Mythology: The Masks of God. Harmondsworth: Penguin.

Casement P (1985) On Learning from the Patient. London: Routledge.

Casement, P. (2002). Learning from our Mistakes: Beyond Dogma in Psychoanalysis and Psychotherapy. Hove: Brunner-Routledge.

Cassius, J. (1975) Body Scripts. Published privately.

Chiaromonte, N (1968) cit. per Roszak T (1971) The Making of a Counter Culture. London: Faber.

Clarkson P (1992) Transactional Analysis Psychotherapy: An Integrated Approach. London: Routledge.

Clarkson P (1993) On Psychotherapy. London: Whurr.

Clarkson P (1995) The Therapeutic Relationship. London: Whurr.

Cooper CL, Bowles D (1977) Hurt or Helped? London: HMSO.

Corey G (1986) The Theory and Practice of Psychotherapy. Pacific Grove Calif: Brooks Cole.

Davis JS (1981) Counselor licensure: overskill? Personal and Guidance Journal 60; 83–5.

Delisle G (1999) Personality Disorders. Montreal: CIG Press, Les Editions du Reflet.

Dychtwaid K (1986). Bodymind. Los Angeles: Tarcher.

Edgar D, Barnes M (1979) Mary Barnes. London: Methuen.

Egan G (1994) The Skilled Helper. Pacific Grove Calif: Brooks/Cole.

Eiden B (2002) Application of post-Reichian body psychotherapy: a Chiron perspective. In Staunton T (ed.) Body Psychotherapy. Hove: Brunner-Routledge, pp. 27–55.

Erskine R, Moursund J (1998) Integrative Psychotherapy in Action. New York: The Gestalt Journal Press.

Erskine R, Moursund J, Troughtman R (1999) Beyond Empathy. New York: Brunner/Mazel.

Fiedler FE (1950) A comparison of therapeutic relationships in psychoanalytic, non-directive, and Adlerian therapy. Journal of Consulting Psychology 14: 239–45.

Fleming P (1998) Contribution Training. London: The Pellin Institute.

Frankl VE (1959) Man's Search for Meaning. New York: Beacon Press.

Fromm E (1962) The Art of Loving. London: Unwin Books.

Gale D (1990) What is Psychodrama? Loughton: Gale Centre Publications.

Gelso CJ, Carter JA (1994) Components of the psychotherapy relationship: their interaction and unfolding during treatment. Journal of Consulting Psychology 41(3): 296–306.

Gladstone G (2002) Groups: a necessary good. Self and Society 30(2): 13–19.

Goulding R, Goulding M (1978) The Power is in the Patient. San Francisco: TA Press.

Grand IJ, Johnson DH (eds) (1998) The Body in Psychotherapy (Inquiries in Somatic Psychology. San Francisco: North Atlantic.

Greenberg IA (1975) Psychodrama. London: Souvenir Press.

Grof S, Grof C (1991) The Stormy Search for Self Understanding and Living with Spiritual Emergency. London: Thorsons, pp. 89–121.

Gross SJ (1977) Professional disclosure: an alternative to licensure. Personal and Guidance Journal 55: 586–8.

Gross SJ (1978) The myth of professional licensing. American Psychologist 33: 1009–16.

Hastings A (1999) Transpersonal Psychology: The Fourth Force. In Moss D (ed.) Humanistic and Transpersonal Psychology: An Historical and Biographical Sourcebook. Westport Conn: Greenwood.

Heimler E (1967) Mental Illness and Social Work. Harmondsworth: Penguin.

Heimler E (1975) Survival in Society. London: Weidenfield & Nicolson.

Heron J (1990) Helping the Client. London: Sage Publications.

Hillman J (1975b) Loose Ends: Primary Papers in Archetypal Psychology. Dallas Tex: Spring Publications.

Hogan DB (1979) The Regulation of Psychotherapists: A Handbook of State Licensure Laws (4 vols). Cambridge Mass: Ballinger.

Horvath AO, Greenberg LS (1994) The Working Alliance: Theory, Research and Practice. London: Wiley.

Hubble MA, Duncan BL, Miller SD (1999) The Heart and Soul of Change : What Works in Therapy. Washington: APA.

Humanistic and Integrative Psychotherapy Section (HIPS) of UK Council for Psychotherapy (2001) Policy Statement on Dual Relationships. London: UKCP.

Hycner R (1993) Between Person and Person. New York: The Gestalt Journal Press.

Illich I (1971) Celebration of Awareness. London: Calder & Boyars.

Johnson SM (1994) Character Styles. New York/London: WW Norton & Company.

Jones D (ed.) (1987) Bhagwan, trick or treat. Self and Society XV(5): 202–36.

Jones D (ed.) (1994) Innovative Therapy. Buckingham: Open University Press.

Josselson R (1996) The Space Between Us. London: Sage.

Jourard S (1971) The Transparent Self. New York: Van Nostrand Reinhold.

Joyce P, Sills C (2001) Skills in Gestalt Counselling and Psychotherapy. London: Sage.

Kahn M (1991) Between Therapist and Client; the New Relationship. New York: Freeman & Co.

Keleman S (1979). Somatic Reality. Berkeley: Center Press.

Kepner J (1987) Body Process – A Gestalt Approach to Working with the Body in

Kernberg O (1979) Object Relations Theory and Clinical Psychoanalysis. New York:

Kottler (1990) On Being a Therapist. Oxford: Jossey-Bass Inc.

Kovel JA (1976) Compete Guide to Therapy. Harmondsworth: Penguin.

Kurtz R (1990) Body-Centered Psychotherapy – The Hakomi Method. Mendocino Calif: Life Rhythm.

Laing RD (1967) The Politics of Experience. London: Penguin.

Lake F (1966) Clinical Theology. London: Darton, Longman & Todd.

Lee R, Wheeler G (1996) The Voice of Shame. London: Jossey-Bass.

Lieberman MA, Yalom, ID, Miles MB (1973) Encounter Groups: First Facts. New York: Basic Books.

Liss J (1974) Free to Feel. London: Wildwood Press.

Little M (1987) Psychotic Anxieties and Containment; A Personal Record of an Analysis with Winnicott. London: Aronson.

Lowen A (1958) The Language of the Body. New York: Collier Macmillan.

Lowen A (1975) Bioenergetics. London: Arkana.

Luborsky L, Singer B, Luborsky L (1975) Comparative studies of psychotherapies: is it true that 'Everyone has won and must have prizes?' Archives of General Psychiatry 32: 995–1008.

MacInnes C (1967) Old youth and young. Encounter (September 1967).

Manship D (1967) Learning to Live. Oxford: Pergamon.

Maslow A (1962) Toward a Psychology of Being. New York: Harper & Row.

Maslow A (1970) Motivation and Personality. 2 edn. New York: Harper & Collins.

Masson J (1990) Against Therapy. London: Fontana.

McEwan I (2001) Only love and then oblivion. Love was all they had to set against their murders. Guardian (24 September).

Mindell A (1989) River's Way: The Process Science of the Dreambody. London: Arkana.

Moreno J (1934) Who Shall Survive? New York: Beacon Hill.

Moss D (ed.) (1999) Humanistic and Transpersonal Psychology: An Historical and Biographical Sourcebook. Westport Conn: Greenwood.

Mowbray R (1995) The Case against Psychotherapy Registration. London: Trans Marginal Press.

Northrup C (1998) Women's Bodies, Women's Wisdom: Creating Physical and Emotional Health and Healing. New York: Bantam.

Nouwen HJM (1994) The Wounded Healer. London: Darton, Longman & Todd.

O'Donohue J (1998) Eternal Echoes. London: Bantam.

Packard V (1957) The Hidden Persuaders. New York: Random House.

Perls F, Hefferline R, Goodman P (1951/1994) Gestalt Therapy: Excitement and Growth in the Human Personality. New York: The Gestalt Journal Press.

Perls FS (1971) Gestalt Therapy Verbatim. Moab: Real People Press (Bantam).

Polster E, Polster M (1974) Gestalt Therapy Integrated: Contours of Theory and Practice. New York: Random House.

Prichett S, Erskine-Hill P (eds) (2002) Education! Education! Education! London: Inprint Academic/Higher Education Foundation.

Psychotherapy. New York: Gestalt Institute of Cleveland Press.

Pugh D (1965) T-group training from the point of view of organisational theory. In Whitaker G (ed.) T-group Training. Oxford: Blackwell, 1965.

Reason P, Rowan J (eds) (1981) Human Inquiry: A Sourcebook of New Paradigm Research. Chichester: John Wiley & Sons.

Reich W (1942) The Function of the Orgasm. New York: Orgone Institute Press.

Reich W (1949) Character Analysis. New York: Orgone Institute Press/Vision.

Reich W (1951) The Sexual Revolution. London: Vision Press.

Rice A (1965) Learning for Leadership. London: Tavistock Publications.

Rogers C (1950) Client-centred Therapy. Boston: Houghton & Mifflin.

Rogers C (1961) On Becoming a Person. London: Constable.

Rogers C (1969) Encounter Groups. London: Penguin.

Rosenberg J (1985) Body, Self and Soul – Sustaining Integration. Atlanta: Humanics.

Roszak T (1971) The Making of a Counter Culture. London: Faber.

Roszak T (1981) Person/Planet. London: Granada Publishing.

Rowan J (1976) Ordinary Ecstasy: Humanistic Psychology in Action. 1 edn. London: Routledge & Kegan Paul.

Rowan J (1983) The Reality Game: A Guide to Humanistic Counselling and Therapy. 1 edn. London: Routledge & Kegan Paul.

Rowan J (1987) A Guide to Humanistic Psychology. London: Association of Humanistic Psychology.

Rowan J (2001) Ordinary Ecstasy. 3 edn. London: Routledge & Kegan Paul.

Rutter P (1989) Sex in the Forbidden Zone. London: Mandala.

Schneider KJ, Bugental JFT, Pierson JF (eds) (2001) The Handbook of Humanistic Psychology. London: Sage Publications.

Schutz WC (1967) Joy. Harmondsworth: Penguin.

Schutz WC (1973) Elements of Encounter. Big Sur Calif: Joy Press.

Searles HF (1993) Concrete and Metaphorical Thinking in the Recovering Schizophrenic Patient in Collected Papers on Schizophrenia and Related Subjects. London: Karnac.

Shaffer J, Galinsky M (1974) Models of Group Therapy and Sensitivity Training. New York: Prentice Hall.

Sinay S (1998) Gestalt for Beginners. New York: Writers and Readers Publishing Inc.

Southgate J, Randall R (1989) The Barefoot Psychoanalyst. London: Gale.

Stafford-Clark D (1952) Psychiatry Today. Harmondsworth: Penguin.

Staunton T (ed.) (2002) Body Psychotherapy. Hove: Brunner-Routledge.

Steiner C (1975) Scripts People Live. New York: Bantam Books.

Steiner C (1982) The Other Side of Power. New York: Grove Publications.

Stevens J (1971) Awareness: Exploring, Experimenting, Experiencing. Utah: Real People Press.

Stewart I, Joines V (1987) TA Today: A New Introduction to Transactional Analysis. Nottingham: Lifespace.

Szasz T (1972) The Myth of Mental Illness. St Albans: Granada.

Tallentyre SG (pseudonym for Hall EB) (1907) The Friends of Voltaire. London: Smith Elder.

Tillich P (1948) The Shaking of the Foundations. New York: Charles Scribner's Sons.

Torronto E (2002) A clinician's response to physical touch on the psychoanalytic setting. International Journal of Psychotherapy 7(1): 69–81.

Totton N (1998) Mind and Body in Psychoanalysis. London: Rebus Press.

UK Assocation for Humanistic Psychology Practitioners Handbook (2003) London: UKAHPP.

Wahl B (2001) Rethinking humanistic therapy. Self and Society 29(4): 5–12.

Wampold BE (2001) The Great Psychotherapy Debate. New Jersey: Lawrence Erlbaum Associates.

West W (1994) Post-Reichian therapy. In Jones D (ed.) Innovative Therapy: A

Whitaker C (1989) Midnight Musings of a Family Therapist. New York: WW Norton & Co.

Whitton E (1992) What is Transactional Analysis? Loughton: Gale Publications.

Whitton E (1998) What do humanistic practitioners really believe? Self and Society 26(3): 7–9.

Yalom ID (1980) Existential Psychotherapy. New York: Basic Books.

Yalom ID (1989) Love's Executioner and Other Tales of Therapy. London: Penguin

Yalom ID (2001) The Gift of Therapy. New York: HarperCollins.

Yontef G (1993) Awareness, Dialogue, and Process: Essays on Gestalt Therapy. New York: Gestalt Journal Press.

Resources

Humanistic Schools and Methods of Psychotherapy

Humanistic therapy, as a generic term, covers a range of different methods. It is important to state that no method in itself is humanistic. It may have a theory that fits humanistic psychology but it is the way the therapist uses himself and his training that is humanistic. It is also important to stress that humanistic is not limited to these methods or graduates of the agencies that emanate from them. There are a number of therapies that are closely associated with the humanistic movement but which are derived from other sources. This appendix sets out the main forms of therapy that are identified as 'humanistic', with some key texts for further study.

Bioenergetics

Boedella D (1985) Wilhelm Reich, The Evolution of His Work. London: Arkana.
Lowen, A (1976) Bioenergetics. London: Coventure.
Reich W (1949) Character Analysis. New York: Orgone Institute Press.

Boyesen

Southwell, C (1988) The Gerda Boyesen Method: Biodynamic Therapy. In Rowan J, Dryden W (eds) Innovative Therapy in Britain. Milton Keyes: Open University Press.

Co-counselling

Heron, J (1974) Reciprocal Counselling. Guildford: Human Potential Research Project.
Jackins, H (1965) The Human Side of Human Beings. New York: Norton.
Southgate J, Randall, R (1989) The Barefoot Psychoanalyst. Loughton: Gale.

Core process and polarity therapy

Donnington L (1994) Core process psychotherapy: In Jones D (ed.) Innovative
    Therapy: A Handbook. Buckingham: Open Unversity Press, pp. 51–67.
Sills F (1990) The Polarity Process. London: Element Books.

Encounter

Shaffer J, Galinsky, D (1974) Models of Group Therapy. Englewood Cliffs:
    Prentice-Hall.
Schutz, W (1989) Joy: Twenty Years Later. Berkeley: Ten Speed Press.
Rogers C (1969) Encounter Groups. Harmonsworth: Penguin.

Existential therapy

Deurzen E van (2002) Existential Counselling and Psychotherapy in Practice. 2
    edn. London: Sage.
Laing RS (1967) The Politics of Experience. Harmondsworth: Penguin.
Yalom I (1980) Existential Psychotherapy. New York: Basic Books.

Gestalt

Fagan J, Shepherd IL (eds) (1970) Gestalt Therapy Now. Palo Alto: Science and
    Behaviour.
Perls FS (1971) Gestalt Therapy Verbatim. Moab: Real People Press.
Stevens, B (1970) Don't Push the River. Moab: Real People Press.

Person-centred therapy

Mearns D, Thorne B (1988) Person-Centred Counselling in Action. London: Sage.
Rogers C (1951) Client Centred Therapy. Boston: Houghton Mifflin.
Rogers C (1961) On Becoming a Person. London: Constable.

Postural integration

Painter J (1986) Deep Bodywork and Personal Development. Mill Valley:
    Bodymind Books.

Primal integration

Grof S (1975) Realms of the Unconscious. New York: Viking Press.
Lake, F (1986) Clinical Theology (abridged M Yeomans). London: Darton,
    Longman & Todd.
Mowbray R, Brown J (1994) Primal integration. In Jones D (ed.) Innovative
    Therapy: A Handbook. Buckingham: Open University Press, pp. 57–67.

Psychodrama

Gale D (1990) What is Psychodrama? Loughton: Gale Publications.
Greenberg I (1974) Psychodrama, Theory and Therapy. London: Souvenir.
Karp, M, Holmes P, Tauvon K (eds) (1998) The Handbook of Psychodrama. London: Routledge.
Moreno J (1964, 1966, 1969) Psychodrama. Vols 1–3. New York: Beacon House.

Psychosynthesis

Assigioli R (1965) Psychosynthesis. London: Turnstone Press.
Ferrucci P (1990) What We May Be. London: Acquarian Press.
Whitmore D (1991) Psychosynthesis Counselling in Action. London: Sage.

Transactional analysis

Berne E (1961) Transactional Analysis in Psychotherapy. New York: Grove Press.
Berne, E (1972) What Do You Say After You Say Hello? New York: Grove Press.
Goulding R, Goulding M (1979) Changing Lives through Redecision Therapy. New York: Brunner/Mazel.

Transpersonal psychotherapy

Maslow A (1973) The Farther Reaches of Human Nature. Harmondsworth: Penguin.
Rowan J (1993) The Transpersonal: in Psychotherapy and Counselling. London: Routledge.
Wilbur K (1997) The Eye of Spirit. Boston: Shambhala.

Journals

Journal of Humanistic Psychology, Sage Publications, 2455 Teller Road, Thousand Island Oaks CA91320, USA.
Self and Society AHP(B) BM Box 3582, London WC1N 3XX.
The Family Therapy Networker, 7705 13th Street NW, Washington DC 20012, USA.

Addresses

Association for Humanistic Psychology, 1516 Oak Street, 320A, Alameda CA94501, USA.
UK Association of Humanistic Psychology Practitioners. BCM AHPP, London WC1N 3XX. Web site: www.ahpp.org
Association for Humanistic Psychology in Britain, BM Box 3582, London WC1N 3XX. Web site: www.ahpb.org.uk
UK Council for Psychotherapy, 167–169 Great Portland Street, London W1W 5PF. Web site: www.psychotherapy.org.uk

Index